Kirtland Elders' Quorum Record

Kirtland Elders' Quorum Record

1836-1841

Edited by

Lyndon W. Cook

Milton V. Backman, Jr.

Distinctive Mormon Documents Series

Grandin Book Company
Provo, Utah

ISBN 0-910523-10-X

Printed in the United States of America

Contents

Preface

The Kirtland Elders' Quorum Record is an official Church minutebook kept during a formative period in the history of Mormonism. It contains fifty-five handwritten pages of minutes for the years 1836 through 1841. Nearly all meetings of the elders' quorum were held in the Kirtland Temple. The clerks who recorded most of these minutes were Evan M. Greene, Warren Smith, and Otis Hobert. Three other clerks—Alexander Cheney, John Gaylord, and John Norton—served only for brief periods of time.

The Elders' Quorum Record has not previously been published. These minutes were not used in the preparation of the Prophet Joseph Smith's *History of the Church* nor have they been used in any other official history of the Church. Scholars have overlooked this important informative source of Mormon history. A major reason for this neglect was that the document remained in Ohio for many years and was not accessible to the Prophet when he dictated the Church's history at Nauvoo. Later, this manuscript became the property of the Reorganized Church of Jesus Christ of Latter Day Saints.

The Kirtland Elders' Quorum Record commences in January 1836 when the elders living in and near Kirtland formally organized with a president, a clerk and counselors. Minutes of their meetings were taken for nearly three years, until late 1838. Increased persecution caused the elders to discontinue meeting regularly.

After the expulsion of the Saints from Missouri, the Mormon population in Kirtland experienced a rebirth as new converts, repentant apostates and displaced members sought physical protection and religious unity. After a hiatus of more than a year, the elders in Kirtland resumed their regular quorum activities, including keeping minutes of their meetings.

For a brief time, Church activities in Kirtland began to flourish. However, this renewed interest in Kirtland as a center place of Zion did not continue. Realizing the futility of supporting two competing Church centers, the Prophet insisted that the Kirtland Stake be abandoned. The final minutes of the Elders' Quorum—October 1841—reflect this decision. Even so, Kirtland continued to serve as a gathering place for Latter-day Saints until the mid-1840s.

Partly because there are so few official Church minutebooks for the Kirtland era, this record is an important and valuable document. More than three hundred male members of the Church participated in the meetings of the Kirtland Elders' Quorum. For purely biographical and genealogical reasons, the record is a treasure. (A biographical index is included in the book.)

However, the record's importance extends beyond being an important source of biographical data. From this work we view the elders' quorum of the early Church as it functioned, learned and grew. The quorum was actively involved in a wide spectrum of duties and responsibilities—from authority problems and administrative precedents to organizational policies and theological questions. Apparent through all of this manuscript is the obvious faith of the early Saints who desired to do right and who demonstrated unusual religious zeal in furthering the message of the Restoration. Significantly, this record provides a broader understanding of Mormon history—a microcosm of the larger Church.

There are other significant contributions of this minutebook. Many activities of the Prophet (not recorded elsewhere) are found here. Also there are descriptions of meetings of temple anointings and other sacred preparations for the solemn assembly and spiritual endowment in the Kirtland Temple. These priesthood rituals will naturally be compared and contrasted with temple ceremonies introduced at Nauvoo.

Like other early Church minutebooks (for example, the Kirtland Council Minute Book, the Kirtland Seventies Record, the Kirtland Revelation Book, and the Far West Record), the kinds of meetings found in the Elders' Quorum Record are more diverse than the title implies. The record also includes minutes of meetings of the Kirtland High Council, the expansion of the Seventies Quourm at Kirtland and other priesthood conferences convened at that place.

During the years 1836-1837 the Kirtland quorum of elders concerned itself solely with ordinations and problems of its members. However, after the departure from Kirtland by the Prophet and many of the other church leaders, this quorum became the only organized priesthood body in Ohio. Therefore, the group began to take on general leadership and administrative responsibilities for the Church in that region, responsibilities which would normally be taken care of by the First Presidency or High Council. For these reasons, the minutes provide a key to understanding events that transpired in Kirtland after the general emigration of the Saints from Ohio and before the discontinuance of the Kirtland Stake.

Sincere appreciation is extended to the RLDS Library-Archives for granting permission to make these minutes available in printed form.

A
Record of
the first quorurum
of Elders
belonging to the Church of
Christ:
in Kirtland
Geauga Co.
Ohio.

15 January 1836

A meeting being called, by the first Presidency of the Church of Latter Day Saints; at the Lord's house[2] in Kirtland: to fill up vacancies in the several quorums. At this meeting, Alvah Beman,[3] was chosen by a unanimous voice of the acting quorums: and ordained President of the quorum of Elders in Kirtland: belonging to the Church of Latter Day Saints.[4]

---

[1]The clerk numbered each of the first eight meetings.

[2]That is, the Kirtland Temple.

[3]Alvah Beman (1775-1837) of Livonia, New York, had long been an intimate friend of Joseph Smith's. In western New York, Beman had helped young Joseph preserve the plates of the Book of Mormon from enemies and on one occasion had concealed them under the hearth in his home (Parley P. Pratt, *Autobiography of Parley P. Pratt*, Parley P. Pratt, Jr. ed. [New York: Russell Bros., 1874], p. 110).

Only a week before this meeting Beman had come to Kirtland to attend the solemn assembly. Apparently he was planning to remove to western Missouri after the dedication of the Kirtland Temple and the solemn assembly in March 1836 (see Joseph Smith, Diary, 16 November 1835 and 13 January 1836, cited in Dean C. Jessee, ed., *The Personal Writings of Joseph Smith* [Salt Lake City: Deseret Book Company, 1984], pp. 85, 89, 129, 134). However, those plans were radically modified when as a result of this meeting he was called to preside over the elders in Kirtland.

[4]An account of this meeting is recorded in the Diary of Joseph Smith, under the same date:

> At the council room in the Chapel [I] organized the authorities of the church agreeably to their respective office in the same, I then made some observation respecting the order of the day, and the great responsibility we are under to transact all our buisness, in righteousness before God, inasmuch as our desisions will have a bearing upon all mankind and upon all generations to come . . . .
>
> Eld[e]r Alva Beemon, was nominated and seconded to officiate as president of the Elders in Kirtland Elder Beemon arose and asked permission to speak, and made the following remarks— Brethren you know that I am . . . old and ignorant and kneed

much instructions, but I wish to do the will of the Lord— The vote of the several authorities was then called and carried unanimously. (Ibid., pp. 132, 134).

On the same occasion, William Cowdery was chosen to preside over the priests in Kirtland, Oliver Olney was called to preside over the teachers, and Ira Bond was named president of the deacons. (See also "Kirtland Council Minute Book," pp. 203-4, Church Archives.) Under the same date, Oliver Cowdery recorded: "The several Quorams of the authorities of the Church met today, and transacted important business preparatory to the endowment" ("Oliver Cowdery Sketch Book," Church Archives).

21 January 1836

2

On the 21st of Jan. 1836, according to appointment the Presidents met at the house of the Lord, and Alvah Beman was anointed to the office where unto he had been ordained.[1]
Notes: The meetings for ordination commence on page[2]

---

[1] The Joseph Smith Diary, for this date (as cited in Jessee, *Writings of Joseph Smith*, pp. 147-48) provides these details of elders' quorum activities:

The president of each quorum then annointed the heads of his colleagues, each in his turn beginning, at the eldest

The vision of heaven was opened to these also, some of them saw the face of the Saviour, and others were ministered unto by holy angels, and the spirit of prop[h]esy and revelation was poured out in mighty power, and loud hosanahs and glory to God in the highest, saluted the heavens for we all communed with the h[e]avenly host's,— and I saw in my vision all of the presidency in the Celestial Kingdom of God, and, many others who were present

Our meeting was opened by singing and prayer offered up by the head of each quorum, and closed by singing and invoking the benediction of heaven with uplifted hands, and retired between one and 2. oclock in the morning.

(For the complete Joseph Smith Diary account of this evening meeting, see Ibid., pp. 145-48.)

Oliver Cowdery tersely summarized the remarkable spiritual manifestations of that evening by saying that what occurred was "too great to be described [in his diary], therefore, I only say, that the heavens were opened to many, and great and marvelous things were shown" ("Oliver Cowdery Sketch Book," under date). President Beman soon was "tempted to doubt" the reality or validity of some of the spiritual happenings of that meeting. However, two days later he "made an humble confession & asked forgiveness of the [leaders] whi[c]h was joyfully given— & the old man said he would try to resist Satan in future" (Joseph Smith, Diary, 23 January 1836, cited in Jessee, *Writings of Joseph Smith*, p. 149).

[2] No page number was supplied in the original record. See the ordination records which begin with the 26 January 1836 entry.

25 January 1836

3

Kirtland Jan. 25th A.D. 1836

This evening a meeting, of Elders, was [called] by the president of said quorum, to instruct them, that they may prepare themselves for the holy anointing.[1]

The meeting being duly organized, Presidents, Sidney Rigdon, F. G. Williams, and Hyrum Smith, were chosen to give the said instructions.

firstly: opened by prayer and then proceeded.

2ndly: The presidents ordained and blessed according to the blessings of the Sons of Zion. Reuben McBride blessed; Tho[mas]-. Hayes, Addision Greene, Benj. Gifford, and Albert Brown blessed and ordained; Benj. Winchester ordained.

3rdly: They gave instructions concerning purification.[2]

4thly: The president of the Elders [Alvah Beman] chose his counsel. Eld. R[euben]. Hadlock was chosen first counselor and Elder J[ohn]. Morton was chosen second counselor, by an unanimous vote.

5thly: President Beman organized the quorum according to age, and take their names.

6thly: The Elders organized into bodies of twelve to make preparations for the Holy anointing.

7thly: Meting adjourned untill the 28th to meet at the same place.

---

[1]The "holy anointing" was part of a complex of sanctifying ordinances intended to prepare the brethren to receive a spiritual outpouring known in Kirtland as "an endowment of power."

[2]"Purification" was one of the ordinances which prepared the brethren for the "endowment." It consisted of having one's body washed and bathed with cinnamon-perfumed whiskey and later washing one's own body with pure water and perfume. Cf. D&C 89:7.

28 January 1836[1]

4

Kirtland Jan. 28th A.D. 1836

This evening met at the house of the Lord; the quorum of Elders to receive their anointing; and the meeting being organized by prayer the High presidency proceeded;

1stly.   To anoint president [Alvah] Beman's cou[n]selors.

2ndly.   President Beman anointed twenty four Elders; (Viz) Jonathan Stevens, Wm. Draper, Hezekiah Fisk, Edmund Bosley, James Webb, Isaac McWithey, Samuel Canfield, John Gould, Alpheus Cutler, Elijah Cheney, Stephen Starks, Joel McWithey, Samuel Phelps, Ezra Thornton, Selah J. Griffing,[2] Shadrach Roundy, Zerah Pulsifer, King Follett, Joseph Rose, Robert Culberson, Gideon Olmsby,[3] John Young, jun., Sam. Newcomb, and Blake Baldwin: and the Lord poured out his spirit, and some spake with tongues and prophecied. Oh the wonderous blessings of the God of Israel.

3rdly.   After the anointing the presidents received the sum of consecration, (ex[tende]d [until the] 30th) to defray the expenses of the anointing.

4thly.   Meeting adjourned untill Sat. the 30th at the same place, and closed by prayer.

---

[1]The Prophet's diary records the following about this meeting held in the attic of the Kirtland Temple:

> In the evening met the quorems of High Priests in the west room of the upper loft of the Lord,s house & in company with my council of the presidency— consecrated & anointed the cou[n]sellors of the President of the High priesthood & having instructed them & set the quorem in order I left them to perform the holy anointing— & went to the quorem of Elders in the other end of the room. I assisted in anointing the counsellors of the President of the Elders & gave them the instruction necessary for the occasion & left the President & his council to anoint the Elders while I should go to the adjoining room & attend to organizing & instructing of the quorem of the Seventy (Joseph Smith, Diary, 28 January 1836, cited in Jessee, *Writings of Joseph Smith*, p. 150).

[2]Selah J. Griffin.
[3]Gideon Ormsby.

30 January 1836[1]

5

Kirtland Jan. 30th 1836

This evening, ~~the~~ president [Alvah] Beman with the Elders of the quorum met at the house of the Lord. The meeting was opened by singing, and prayer, and president Beman proceeded to anoint twenty four; (Viz) Ja[mes]. Foster, Artemus Millett, Salmon Gee, Nat. Milliken, Gad Yale, Oliver Granger, Josiah Butterfield, Elias Benner, Uzziel Stevens, Tho. Burdick, Elijah Fordam, Robert Rathbone, Hiram Dayton, Giles Cook, J[ohn]. E. Page, J[oel]. H. Johnson, Wm. Tenny jr., Daniel Wood, Edmund Marvin, Geo. Morey, Reuben McBride, M. C. Davis,[2] Almon Shermon, I[saac]. H. Bishop; and the president and cou[n]sel gave such instructions as were necessary; and the meeting adjourned by prayer untill the 1st of Feb.

---

[1]On this same day, at a council of the presidency of the Church, it was "resolved that no one be ordained to an office in the Church in Kirtland without the voice" of that quorum assembled. Also that "Alvah Beaman, the President of the Elders, be directed to give to the Presidents of the Church, a list of the names of the several Elders comprising his quorum and all other Elders in Kirtland not belonging to any quorum now established" ("Kirtland Council Minute Book," p. 137).

[2]Marvel or Maleum C. Davis.

1 February 1836[1]

6

Kirtland Feb. 1st A D. 1836

The quorum met according to appointment and being duly organized proceeded to business.

The Pres. [Alvah Beman] anointed 26 and proceeded to other business: several petitions were presented for prayers in behalf of those who were sick. Some instructions given and dismissed with singing and prayer.

---

[1]Although the Elders' Quorum Record does not mention it, the Prophet Joseph Smith was in attendance in the Temple this evening and aided them in their preparation for the endowment:

> [I]n the evening attended to the organizing of the quorems of High priests— Elders— Seventy & Bishops in the uper rooms of the house of the Lord & after blessing each quorem in the name of the Lord I left them & returned home (Joseph Smith, Diary, 1 February 1836, cited in Jessee, *Writings of Joseph Smith*, p. 155).

4 February 1836

7

Kirtland Feb. 4th

Met according to appointment and being duly organized proceeded with the anointing; and Elder [Reuben] Hadlock in forming them to send up their petitions to the Lord of heaven and earth.

Twenty three were anointed and we proceeded to other business.

Agreed to meet to confess one to another[1] and pray one for another.

Closed by singing and prayer.

------

[1]Confession of sins was part of the preparation for the spiritual endowment.

6 February 1836[1]

8

Feb. 6th

Met to proceed with the anointing of the Elders of the Most High.

Counselor [John] Morton organizied those who were anointed in order for supplications.[2]

President [Alvah] Beman finished the anointing.

The first presidency came and sealed our anointing by prayer and shout of Hosanna.

The first counselor [Reuben Hedlock] organized those who had been anointed in order for supplications.

They gave us some instructions and left us. President Beman spake to the assembly: several spoke and there seemed to be a cloud of darkness in the room. Press. O[liver]. Cowdery & H[yrum]. Smith came and gave some instructions and and the cloud was broken and some shouted, Hosanna and others spake with tongues. The first president (J. Smith j[u]n) returned and reprimanded us for our evil deeds which was the cause of our darkness.

He prophesied saying this night the key is turned to the nations; and the angel John is about commencing his mission to prophesy

before kings, and rulers, nations tongues and people.[3]
The assembly was dismissed with prayer.

---

[1]The Diary of Joseph Smith also records the events of the anointed quorums on this day:

> Saturday 6 called the anointed together to receive the seal of all their blessings. The High Priests & Elders in the council room as usual— The Seventy with the Twelve in the second room & the Bishop in the 3— I laboured with each of these quorems for some time to bring [them] to the order which God had shown to me which is as follows— first part to be spent in solemn prayer before god without any talking or confusion & the conclusion with a sealing prayer by Pres. Sidney Rigdon when all the quorems are to shout with one accord a solemn hosannah to God & the Lamb with an Amen— amen & amen— & then all take seats & lift up their hearts in silent prayer to God & if any obtain a prophecy or visions to rise & speak that all may be edified & rejoice together I had considerable trouble to get all the quorems united in this order— I went from room to room repeatedly & charged each separately— assuring them that it was according to the mind of God yet notwithstanding all my labour— while I was in the east room with the Bishops quorems I f[e]lt by the spirit that something was wrong in the quorem of Elders in the west room— & I immediately requested Pres. O. Cowdery & H. Smith to go in & see what was the matter— The quorem of Elders had not observed the order which I have given them & were reminded of it by Pres. Carloss Smith & mildly requested to observe order & continue in prayer & requested— some of them replied that they had a teacher of their own & did not wish to be troubled by others this caused the spirit of the Lord to withdraw This interrupted the meeting & this quorem lost th[e]ir blessing in a great measure—
> the other quorems were more careful (Joseph Smith, Diary, 6 February 1836, cited in Jessee, *Writings of Joseph Smith*, pp. 156-57).

[2]The "supplications" were part of the preparation for the endowment. Specifically, they consisted of silent prayer by the united quorum after which the Church presidency joined them for a prayer of sealing which included a united shout of "hosannah to God & the Lamb" and "Amen, Amen, and Amen."

[3]This reference to the Apostle John is not found in the Diary of Joseph Smith. See Revelation 10:10-11, and D&C 77:14.

8 February 1836[1]

Feb. 8th

Met at the Lord's house and one was anointed, and the presidents of the seventy called those by name chosen for the second seventy;[2] adjourned by prayer.

---

[1]Note that the clerk discontinued numbering each meeting.

[2]That is, the second quorum of seventy was called directly from President Beman's quorum. Most of them had received their anointing in preparation for the endowment. (See "General Record of the Seventies, Book A," Church Archives, pp. 6-8.)

11 February 1836

Feb. 11th

This evening [met] according to adjournment and being duly organized; president [Alvah] Beman gave some instructions respecting the duty of the officers, and made some confession and was followed by president Joseph Smith jr. in giving instruction to the quorum.[1] Pres. Beman proceeded to anoint these Elders, and his counsel organized them for prayer. The Elders continued their confessions a short time, and the presidents of the seventy came and called forth their seventy from our quorum; this being completed we adjourned with prayer.

---

[1]This brief reference to the Prophet Joseph Smith's activities with the elders' quorum is not contained in his diary.

15 February 1836

Kirtland Feb 15th A D. 1836

This evening the quorum met at the house of the Lord and being organized proceeded to confess their fault to one another and pray one for another: meeting adjourned by prayer.

19 February 1836

Feb 19th

The quorum met in the Lord's house, and being organized Pres. [Alvah] Beman anointed two Elders. Elder L[ibbeus]. T. Coons presented the case of Elder E[zra]. Hayes before the quorum.

A bottle of oil was consecrated to the Lord, and meeting dismissed with prayer.

22 February 1836

Feb 22nd

The quorum met and names were presented to carry before the quorums for ordination: business being finished adjourned with prayer.

26 February 1836

Feb. 26th

The quorum met to tell their experience, and the meeting being organized the case of Elder Dean Gould was brought before them: and it being considered the meeting adjourned with prayer.

29 February 1836

Kirtland Feb 29th 1836

This day the quorum met at the Lord's house, and proceeded in telling their experience, and expressing their feelings one to another.

2 March 1836

March 2nd

This evening the Elders met at the Lord's house: the meeting opened by prayer and a hymn was sung; and president [Alvah] Beman proceeded to anoint the following Elders (viz), Richard Howard A[g]e 53, Daniel S. Miles A[g]e 45, Moses Gardner A[g]e 42, David Clough A[g]e 40, Aaron Smith Jr. A[g]e 38, Phinehas H. Young A[g]e 37, Trouman Jackson A[g]e 34, Wm. Wightman A[g]e 28, Reuben Barton A[g]e 24, and Charles Wightman A[g]e 26.[1]

The Brethren were then organized for and sent up their prayers to the father in heaven; the blessings were then sealed by a prayer from the president, and a shout of Hosanna. The Brethren then spake of the goodness of the Lord, and told their feeling[s] and determinations.

The meeting was then dismissed with singing and prayer.

---

[1] Six of these brethren were approved on the 24th of February, 1836, and ordained on the 27th and 28th of the same month ("Kirtland Council Minute Book," pp. 144-45). Because of their relevance, the entries from the "Kirtland Council Minute Book" for these dates have been included. See those dates for these insertions.

4 March 1836

Mar 4th

This evening the Elders met at the Lord's house and being duly organized proceeded to speak one to another as they felt in the Lord. The meeting then dismissed with prayer.

7 March 1836

Kirtland March 7th 1836

This evening the Elders met, and being duly organized, the case of Dean Gould came before the Elders, also Elder [Calvin W.] Stoddard made his confession: ten were also received into the quorum. Dismissed with prayer.

9 March 1836

March 9th

The Elders met, and being duly organized six Elders were anointed, and some spake of the goodness of God, dismissed with prayer.

11 March 1836

March 11th

The Elders met, and being organized, the case of Elder Dean Gould was again brought forward, and president [Alvah] Beman stated to the quorum that Elder D. Gould had not appeared to make his confession but the accusation (I.E.) he behaved in an unchristian like manner was disobedient to his parents &c., and he, Dean, left the house, on the evening of the 7th went into the school house, as testified by Elder Wm Bosley and Mosses Martin, and their went to jumping and behaved himself in an unchristian like manner, and was reproved by them. The quorum then, by vote, withdrew the hand of fellowship from him: again voted to carry his case to the high council of Kirtland: and dismissed with prayer.

16 March 1836

Kirtland March 16, 1836

This evening the Elders met according to appointment, in the Lord's house.

The meeting being duly organized; President [Alvah] Beman consecrated a bottle of oil for the anointing; after which a hymn was sung and he proceeded to anoint Elders Benj. Brown A[g]e 41, James Burnham A[g]e 38, Julius Thompson A[g]e 34, and E. F. Nickerson A[g]e 29.

Elder [Reuben] Hadlock organized them for prayer.

The blessings were then sealed by the President, and the meeting dismissed with prayer.

21 March 1836

March 21st 1836

The quorum [met] for a prayer meeting, and President [Alvah] Beman presided.

25 March 1836

March 25th

The Elders met for a prayer meeting; President [Alvah] Beman presided, two were received into the quorum this evening.

18 March 1836

March 18

The Elders met in the Lord's house; and being duly organized, the following Elders were ordained Joshua Bosley, Erastus Wightman, and Samuel Thompson: and the following ones were anointed, Lorenzo Young, Heman Hyde, John Gaylord, Joshua Bosley, Osmyn M. Duel, Erastus Wightman, Chapman Duncan, Samuel Thompson and Daniel Jackson.[1] Lorenzo Young was delivered to the presidents of the seventies, Prs Smith dismissed.

The meetings [on] the 18, and 19 were handed to me by Elder

Hadlock sepperate from the above and therefor[e] are ent[e]red after the 21st, and 25. E[van] M Greene [clerk]

---

[1]Several of these brethren were approved and ordained at a meeting of the several quorums of the Church on the 17th of March, 1836 (see "Kirtland Council Minute Book," p. 146, which is included in the entry for 17 March 1836 hereafter).

19 March 1836

Kirtland March 19. 1836

This evening the Elder[s] met at the Lord's house, with other quorums of the church. The meeting was opened by singing, and prayer. President Joseph Smith J[u]n.[1] gave some instructions relative to the sealing power, in a short but powerful address.[2]

President S. Rigdon sealed the blessings of the Lord on those who had been anointed, by prayer and with a shout of Hosanna to God and, the Lamb.

Some of the brethren spake of the goodness of the Lord, and President J. Smith jun made some remarks respecting the coming meeting,[3] and gave out some appointments.

Brother Jacobs[4] told his feelings, and the president of the High priests[5] with some of his quorum spake, and the meeting closed with singing and prayer.

---

[1]These minutes contain information concerning the Prophet's activities not included in his own diary.

[2]The "sealing power" had reference to the early Mormon practice of "electing" certain members of the Church to be candidates to the celestial kingdom by the power of the priesthood. Beginning in 1831, High Priests were given the authority to seal up individuals that were identified to them by revelation (D&C 68:12, and *Far West Record: Minutes of The Church of Jesus Christ of Latter-day Saints, 1830-1844* Donald Q. Cannon and Lyndon W. Cook, eds., [Salt Lake City: Deseret Book Company, 1983], pp. 20-21: "Br. Joseph Smith jr. said that the order of the Highpriesthood is that they have power given them to seal up the Saints unto eternal life. And said it was the privilege of every Elder present to be ordained to the Highpriesthood"). This practice was discontinued sometime in 1835 and not resumed until the Nauvoo period, and then only by express permission and direction of the Prophet. The Mormon doctrine of election differed from that of other religious groups in that the Saints believed that a person could fall from grace (by sin) after achieving grace (D&C 20:32) even though he might have been elected or "sealed" up unto eternal life. Such wilful sin would result in being delivered over to the buffetings of Satan.

Note that the use of the word "seal" as it relates to the anointings mentioned above meant that the promises or ordinances were being bound by the holy priesthood, not that these brethren were being sealed up unto eternal life.

³Reference is to the solemn assembly (wherein the brethren were to receive the spiritual endowment). This meeting was held less than two weeks later on the 30th of March, 1836.

⁴Dana or Michael Jacobs.

⁵Don Carlos Smith had been appointed president of the High Priests in Kirtland on the 15th of January, 1836.

26 March 1836

March 26th

This day the Elders met at the Lord's house and being organized the president and counsel proceeded to anoint the following Elders, Jacob Mires A[g]e 53, Michael B. Welton A[g]e 44, Joshua S. Holman A[g]e 41, Jam[es]. Durfee A[g]e 41, John Mackly A[g]e 40, Judah Griffeth A[g]e 46, Michael Barkdell A[g]e 36, Jam[es]. Bradan A[g]e 35, Jeremiah Mackley A[g]e 36, Phinehas Bronson A[g]e 33, Geo[rge]. F. James A[g]e 39, and Reuben C. Wetherby. The blessings were sealed some exhortations given, and meeting closed with prayer.

26 January 1836

The meetings for ordination.

Kirtland Jan. 26th A.D. 1836

The president of the Elders (Alvah Beman) met with his counsel (Reuben Hadlock and John Morton) at the house of Elder [Joseph] Bates Nobles, and the meeting being organized the president ordained his co[u]nsel; and the following Elders (Viz) Sterry Fisk, Gad Yale, James Thompson, Dean Gould, and Geo. Rose. Instructions were given them how to prepare for the holy anointing: and E[van]. M. Greene was chosen for a standing clerk for the quorum. The meeting adjourned with prayer until Wed. 1 oclock P.M.

24 February 1836¹

[Kirtland Feb. 24th 1836

The several quorums met in the House of the Lord, to conclude the business concerning the ordination of official members in the church of Christ, of the Latter Day Saints, also to ordain the following members to the office of Elders in said Church.

Opened by prayer

The names of Wm. Wightman & Charles Wightman were presented and a vote of the whole assembly called and passed unanimously, that they be received. Copeland Hubbards name presented, objections were raised and his name dropped.

Henry Grant	Rejected
Henry Baldwin	"
Moses Tracey	"
John B. Coppentis	"
David Cluff	Received
Buhias Dustin	Rejected
Samuel Hale	"
Truman Jackson	Received
Mahew Hillman	Rejected
Isaac Cleaveland	Rejected
Albert Miner	"
Jamon Aldrich	"
Naman Blodgete	"
Elias Hart	"
Nathan Staker	"
Reuben Barton	Received
Daniel Miles	"
George Dunn	Rejected
John H. Almsby	"
Joel God[d]ard	"
Henry Garrit	"
Willi[a]m Bartler	"

Moses Daily{'s} name presented for the office of the High Priesthood. Vote passed unanimously.

O. Cowdery Orson Hyde & Sylvester Smith were nominated and seconded to write rules and regulations concerning licenses. Vote called and unanimously passed.

Thomas Burdick was nominated and seconded to officiate as Clerk to record licenses. Vote called & unanimously passed. Nominated and seconded that the calls for preaching in the Vic{i}nity round about be attended to under the direction of the 12 {apostles} and the Presidency of the 70. Council adjourned till Thursday evening the 4th of March 1836.

Closed by singing & prayer
W{arren} Parrish Clerk]

---

[1]These minutes are not part of this record but are from the "Kirtland Council Minute Book," pp. 144-45. Because of their importance to this document, they have been included here.

17 March 1836[1]

[Kirtland March 17th 1836

The several quorums met in the House of the Lord for Church business, and after prayer the following names were presented requesting to be ordained (viz.)

John Gaylord{'s} name presented for ordination to the office of an Elder.

Daniel Johnson{'s}	name presented	rejected
Samuel Thomson	"	"
Joseph Ball	"	"
Erastus B. Wightman	"	received
Osmeyn M. Duel	"	"
Chapman Dunken	"	"
Henry Green	"	rejected
Joshua Bosley	"	agreed
Heman Hyde	"	"

Closed by prayer

O. Cowdery Clerk of Conference]

---

[1]These minutes are not part of this record but are from the "Kirtland Council Minute Book," p. 146. Because of their importance to this document, they have been included here.

27 March 1836

Wed 27. 1836.

The president and cou[n]cil met according to appointment, and being organized the following Elders were ordained Gideon Almsby, Blake Baldwin, Amasa Boney, Jonathan Crosby, Wm Gould, Rufus Fisher, Stephen Post, Jonathan Hampton, Chauncy G. Webb, and Wm Miller.

They were instructed how to prepare for the holy anointing. Several exhorted and spake of the goodness of God some spake in tongues, and others interpreted; and meeting was dismissed with prayer. In the evening met again at the same place, and after prayer ordained Dexter Stillman an Elder and dismissed with prayer.

28 March 1836

Thurs. 28

The president and counsel met at Elder [Joseph B.] Nobles' house and ordained Moses Lindsley and gave him instructions, and dismissed with prayer.

30 January 1836

Kirtland Jan. 30th 1836

This day the president and counsel met at the house of Elder Bosley,[1] and being duly organized, ordained Wm Parks an Elder and [gave] him such instructions as were necessary. Dismissed with prayer.

---

[1] Edmund or Joshua Bosley.

27 February 1836

Feb. 27th   the president and counsel met at Elder [Joseph B.] Nobles house, and being organized, ordained the following Elders Trouman Jackson, Wm Wightman and Reuben Barton and gave them instructions and dismissed with prayer.

28 February 1836

28th   We met again and being organized, president [Alvah] Beman's health was poor and he gave the meeting into the hands of counselor [Reuben] Hadlock who proceeded and ordained Daniel S. Miles and David Clough Elders and gave them instructions: the meeting dismissed with prayer.

17 March 1836

March 17th.   The president and counsel met and being organized ordained the eight who had been set apart for Elders: gave them instructions and dismissed with prayer.

14 April 1836

April 14th   The president of the high priests[1] met with his counsel, and president [Alvah] Beman being gone to the east[2] he anointed the following Elders who were received into the quorum by the clerk. Geo[rge]. Burket A[g]e 47, Martin C. Allred A[g]e 29, Harvey Green A[g]e 29, Peter Shirts A[g]e 27, and William O. Clark A[g]e 18.

---

[1]Don Carlos Smith.

[2]President Beman was absent from Kirtland from April to October 1836 (see minutes for 28 October 1836 meeting).

29 April 1836

Minutes of a High Council held in Kirtland April 29 A D. 1836. President Joseph Smith sen. presided.
Introductory prayer & remarks by the pr[e]s.
1. Voted that Elder Oliver Granger be ordained a High Priest.
2. Voted that brother James H. Smith be ordained an Elder.
3. Voted that Priest Lyman Leonard be ordained an Elder.
4. Voted that brother Ebenezer Robinson be ordained an Elder.
5. Voted that Pr[e]s. of Teachers Mayhew Hillman be ordained an Elder.
6. Voted that Priest Jabez Durfee be ordained Elder.
7. Voted that brother James Durfee be ordained an Elder.

8. Voted that Wm. Tenny sen. be ordained a Priest.

9. Voted that Elder Alpheus Cutler be ordained a High Priest.

The above named brethren were ordained and set apart to their several callings and offices as named above, by Pr[e]s Joseph Smith sen. and [high] counselors John Smith and Joseph Coe: and Elder Oliver Granger closed by prayer.

30 April 1836

April 30th   the [High] council met again in the Lord's house and proceeded to anoint the following Elders.[1] Pr[e]s Joseph Smith presided with [high] counselors John Smith and Henry G. Sherwood.

1 James Lake, 2 Lyman Leonard, 3 Perry Durfee, 4 Wm Harris, 5 Wm Barker, 6 Joseph A. Kelting, 7 Lyman Curtis, 8 Ebenezer Robinson, 9 James H. Smith, & 10 Elam Meachan jun.

These Elders with a Priest were anointed in the Lord's house with fasting and washing of feet according to the order given for the endowment of God,[2] in the last days by the Pr[e]s. and assistant.

---

[1]High Priests, particularly members of the Kirtland High Council, presided in these anointing meetings in the absence of President Alvah Beman.

[2]Fasting, washing of feet, and partaking of the Lord's Supper were the final phase of the preparation for the Kirtland "endowment."

14 June 1836

The minutes of a confrence of Elders held in Kirtland June 14th A D. 1836.

After prayer and due inquiry into the character of brother Trouman Gillett Jun. and his qualifications to preach the gospel, it was thought advisable to ordain him to the office of an Elder, and the following Elders were set apart for that to ordain him, W[arren]. A. Cowdery, Leonard Rich, and Hiram Dayton.

26 October 1836

A meeting of the Elders quorum was called on the 26th of Oct. A D. 1836. The meeting was organized by request of Pres. [Alvah] Beaman, with singing, preparatory remarks, and prayer by the Pres:

he also gave an interesting account of the dealings of God with him since our last meeting in the Spring.[1] It was moved and carried that E[van] M Greene should still act as clerk for the quorum.

The Licence of C[alvin]. W. Stodard was presented. Moved and carried, to retain the Licence and not raise our hands against him. Then proceeded to enroll the names of the Elders present who had not been with the quorum: and twenty were received.

The clerk then read the proceedings of H[igh] Council in respect to the Elders quorum during the absence of Pres. [Beman].

Liberty was then given for exhortation, and many spake of the goodness of God, and our souls were blessed with his spirit.

It was moved and carried that our meetings for the winter of [18]36.[18]37 be every Wednesday evening. Meeting adjourned with singing and prayer.

---

[1]See minutes for 14 April 1836.

2 November 1836

Wed. Nov 2nd   met agreeable to adjournment. Organized with singing & prayer.

Enrolled the names of nine Elders, and received the names of four as candidates for Elders. Several spake of the goodness of the Lord. A question was proposed, by Elder I Conkins, respecting the two Priesthood[s], and of what priesthood were Joshua and the prophets: which was answered by the clerk [Evan M. Greene].

Meeting adjourned with prayer.

It was mentioned, this evening, about raising monies for the expenditure of the quorum, but, the council being absent was defered.

9 November 1836

Nov. 9th   met according to appointment. Organized with singing & prayer; Then proceeded to business. Ten names were received as candidates for the ministry.

It was moved and carried that monies be raised by donation for the expenditure of the quorum. Elder Tho. Burdick was chosen treasurer by a full vote. Voted that the now standing quorum pay the present ar[r]erages: also voted that Pres. [Alvah] Beaman request one of the first Presidents[1] to meet and explain the order of the two Priesthoods. Recd one Elders name and closed with singing and prayer.

[1]That is, one of the First Presidency.

16 November 1836

Nov. 16   the quorum met according to appointment in the Lord's house.

Meeting being duly organized; the presidency proceeded, according to a previous vote, to take a collection, to defray the necsesary expenses of the

The presidents of the seventies; then, called the names of those, whom, they had chosen for the 3rd Seventies.[1]

Resolved by a full vote that the meetings of the Elders quorum be conducted in the following manner (Viz) to commence with the oldest and speak & pray in rotation, as their names are called.

Elder [Peter] Shirts [who was ill] then recd the laying on of hands, and meeting adjourned, with singing and prayer.

[1]See "General Record of the Seventies, Book A," 20 December 1836, p. 9.

23 November 1836

No[v] 23.   The Elders quorum met according to appointment. Introductory remarks by the Pres. [Alvah Beman] and opening prayer by Eld. Wm Draper. The names presented for ordination, and one Elder joined the quorum. Meeting adjourned as usual.

30 November 1836

The Elders met according to appointment at the Lord's house in Kirtland Nov. 30 1836. Meeting opened with singing and prayer. Then Pres J. Smith jun. delivered a lecture on the Subject of the Priesthood when he finished liberty was given for speaking.[1] Three

names were presented for ordination. Meeting adjourned with singing and prayer.

---

[1]Because his Kirtland diary ends in April 1836, it does not contain this brief reference
to the Prophet's activities with the Elders' quorum. Consequently, this reference to an address of the Prophet Joseph did not appear in his published *History*.

7 December 1836

The Elders met in the Lord's house Dec 7. Meeting being duly
organized, the Pres. of the Seventies proceeded to call the third
Seventy, sixty four were drawn.

Three names [were] recd for ordination.

Meeting adjourned as usual.

14 December 1836

The Elders quorum met Dec. 14th A D 1836. The meeting was
called to order by the Pr[e]s [Alvah Beman] and opened by singing
and prayer. Some gave in their names for ordination, and counselor
[Reuben] Hadlock and the cl[erk Evan M. Greene] arranged the
names to present to the general council.[1] Many spoke of the goodness
of the Lord and truly we enjoyed his spirit.

Meeting closed with singing and prayer.

---

[1]Names of brethren submitted for ordination to the office of elder were first presented
to the Kirtland High Council for approval.

21 December 1836

The Elder's quorum met Dec 21th A D 1836. and being duly
organized the pres. [Alvah Beman] made some remarks, and the clerk
[Evan M. Greene] read the names of those whom the council[1] set
apart for Elders. next took the names of Elder Mosses R. Norriss
A[g]e 46. Then names for ordination were presented for ordination
Elisha Wright, Hammon H. Hills, Easton Kelsey. Then came forward for ordinations Mathew Allen, John Williams, Wm Wyrick,
and counselor [John] Morton being absent Elder E[dmund]. Bosley

was chosen a counsel[lor] Protem, and proceeded to the ordination.
The meeting then adjourned with singing and prayer.

---

[1]Kirtland High Council.

28 December 1836

The Elders met Dec 28th A D 1836. Organized by prayer, and
the Pres. [Alvah Beman] after making some remarks proceeded to ordain those appointed. Ten were ordained, and counselor [John] Morton gave an exhortation. Recd the name of Elder Benj. S. Wilber.
Then recd names for ordination H[ezekiah]. W. Fisk, Isaac Rogers,
Licander M. Davis, Saml Fowler, Thos. Butterfield, Eleazer King,
Rulen Field, Lorenzo King. Adjourned with singing and prayer.

4 January 1837

The Elders met Jan 4th A D 1837. Opened by prayer and the
brethren continued some time in prayer and then in exhortation.
These names were recd for ordination John Lyons, Cha[rles] N.
Baldwin, Z[enos]. H. Breuster, Isaac Hubbard, Zemira Draper.
Pres. [Alvah] Beman gave appoint[ment] to investigate the duties
of an Elder at our next meeting. Bro. [Peter] Shirts had hands laid on
him again and arose and declared that his pain was removed.[1]
The meeting adjourned as usual.

---

[1]See minutes for 16 November 1836.

11 January 1837

The Elders quorum met [as] usual Jan 11th A D 1837. Meeting
opened with singing and prayer. 2nd The Pres. [Alvah Beman] questioned the quorum in respect to their duty.
3 Elder Corking proposed the following question, is it the duty ~~to
proposed~~ of an Elder to cast out unbelievers from the room when
called to administer to the sick.
4 Father [Joseph] Smith answered as follows, if they are a com-

pany of unbelievers, cast them out but an Elder if humble shall know what is to be done.

5 Elder C. proposed again, if a priest has an appointment and an Elder comes shall he take the lead of that meeting.

6 Answered in the negative.

7 Father Smith proposed, if an Elder traveling come into a church where there is a standing Elder, shall he take the lead of meetings and appoint meetings there without the solici[ta]tion of the other.

8 Answered in the negative.

9 Several of the like questions proposed, and father Smith & pres. Beman gave instruction.

10 Is it the duty of an Elder to lay hands on a sick person without solicitation.

11 Ans. in the negative.

12 Recd names for ordination. Lorenzo D. LaBar[o]n, Albert Minor, Edwin P. Mer[r]iam, Jessee Baker, Orren Cheeney.

13 Elder A[bel]. Lamb came forward and Father [Joseph] Smith took the lead and laid hands on him, and Norman Buel and Elias Wright, and coun[selor Reuben] Hedlock.

Meeting adjourned with prayer.

18 January 1837

The Elders met Jan. 18 A D 1837.

1   Meeting opened with singing & prayer.

2   The pres. [Alvah Beman] made some remarks to the quorum, and reproved them for murmuring ag[a]inst the pres. of the Church[1] by relating a vision.

3   Pres. Hiram Smith addressed us in his usual pathetic and interesting manner, reproving murmuring and [missing record].[2]

---

[1]The problem of "murmuring" against the heads of the Church was apparently widespread at this time (see Journal of Wilford Woodruff, 10 January 1837).

[2]At this point in the record one or more pages of minutes are missing. And owing to the fact that the pagination ends at this point, it impossible to determine the extent of the loss. However, it is probable that the missing text is limited only to a meeting or two in the month of January 1837 since minutes for the month of February 1837 are recorded with the 1838 minutes. The record recommences in the middle of the minutes of an undated meeting at the point where five other items of business had already been discussed (see the following entry).

No Date

6th Pres. Beaman proposed to know how death reigened from Adam to Moses even over those whoo had not Sined.[1]

7th   Elder S[amuel]. Canfield proposed to know who the Shep[h]erd the Stone of Isreal is Spoken off in gen[esis]. 49:22.

8th   Many Spoke of the goo[d]nes of God

9th   Closed by prayer.

---

[1]Romans 5:14.

1 March 1837

March 1st 1837

1st opened with Prayer and proseded to consider the first questi[o]n pr[o]posed by Coun [Reuben] Hedlock that is to know the Duties of an elder Coun Hedlock made some preliminary remarks the Second questi[o]n came forward See romans 5:14 & many remark[s] were made.

2nd Elder [Sampson] Averd made Some remarks & the quorum Joined him in prayer.

3rd   Names of Elders

4th   Names for ordaination David Holman Isaac Cleavland defered the third questi[o]n til next meeting

5th   Coun Hedlock proposed the fol[l]owing to know the power of those Elders Sent forth to bind up the Law and Seal up the testimony.[1]

meeting closed with Sin[g]ing and prayer.

---

[1]D&C 88:84 (compare D&C 109:46 and Isaiah 8:16 which renders the idea: "seal up the law, and bind up the testimony"). Cf. D&C 1:8-9.

15 March 1837

March 15 1837

The Elders quroum met in the Lords house

1st the first questi[o]n agitated was what Dose the Elders Do to bind up the Law and Seal up the testimony.[1]

2nd meeting Closed by sin[g]ing and prayer.

---

[1]See 1 March 1837, note 1.

22 March 1837

March 22 1837

The Elders quorum met in the Lords house

1st   opening prayer by the president of the quorum

2nd   the questi[o]n by Elder S[amuel]. Canfield answer[e]d by Elder [William W.] Spencer[1]

3rd   Elder [Elisha H.] Groves Spoke before the quorum presented a Subscription for the Lords house in the far west.[2]

4th   a charge perfered against Ad[d]ison Green for unchristen like conduct by W[illiam] F Cahoon.

5th   Elders Joined the quorum Freeman Nickerson Geo W Bro[o]kes

6th   the meeting Closed by prayer.

---

[1]See meeting of 18 January 1837.

[2]Groves, on 15 November 1836, was selected a member of a building committee in Missouri to build a temple at Far West (see Cannon and Cook, *Far West Record*, p. 102). After being set apart, Groves "started on that business about the 20 of Dec [1836] traveled through the branches to Kirtland [and] obtained a subscription of $1,500" (Elisha H. Groves, Autobiography, Church Archives).

29 March 1837

March 29 1837

The quorum of Elders met in the Lords house

1st   The meeting op[e]ned by Prayer

2nd   the case [of] Elder Addison Green was brought forward and Charges read as follows (Viz) 1st for Disturbing the Sin[g]ing Sc[h]oll several times 2nd for Swearing and calling the Complainant a liar (Wm F. Cahoon)

3rd   the 1st Charge Denied by Defendant the 2nd ackno[w]loged

4th   after Some remarks a vote was Called to See if Elder Greens

Statement (that Elder Wm Cahoon had lied) was ~~true~~ a Correct Statement or Not. answered in the Negative

5th   it was mooved & Secon[d]ed that a vote be called to know if
they fellowshiped Elder Green answer[e]d in the Negative

6th   Joseph Smith Jr made Some remarks[1] and Notified the Elders
that the Solem assembley was to be Called on the 6[th] of April &
also that those Elders who were Not anointed must be anointed
before that time[2] Also prophised that unless the church acts in ~~perfect~~
greater union than they had for the winter past it Should be Scourged
untill they Should feel it four fold to that of the dispersion of Zion.

7th   after pres Smiths remarks Pres [Alvah] Beaman Notified the
Breatheren that the Council would not be Called before the Solem
assembly

8th   Notis was given ~~to the Elders~~ that the pres would Commence
anointing at the Next meeting
meeting adjourned with Sin[g]ing and prayer.

---

[1]These minutes contain information concerning the Prophet's activities in Kirtland not
included in his published *History*.

[2]The Prophet's remarks refer to a second solemn assembly planned for the 6th of April,
1837. Worthy brethren who were unable to attend the solemn assembly the previous year
were invited to participate in certain purifying ordinances preparatory to receiving a
spiritual endowment of power. These ordinances consisted of (1) washing "head to foot" in
soap and water, (2) washing in clear water and perfumed whiskey, (3) having one's head
anointed with consecrated oil and receiving a blessing by the spirit of prophecy, (4) having
the anointing blessing sealed with uplifted hands (solemn prayer, a sealing prayer, and the
hosannah shout), and (5) washing of faces and feet and partaking of the Lord's Supper.

31 March 1837

The meeting of March 31st 1837 is caried to the bo[t]tom of the
page[1]

---

[1]This is the clerk's notation that the minutes of this meeting appear later and are
recorded out of chronological order.

3 April 1837

April 3rd 1837

The Elders quorum met in the Lords house[1]

1st   meeting opened with an [ad]dress from the pres [Alvah

Rare early photograph of the Kirtland Temple

Lower auditorium of temple, showing the curtains (or "veils") which could be lowered from the ceiling to subdivide the main assembly room

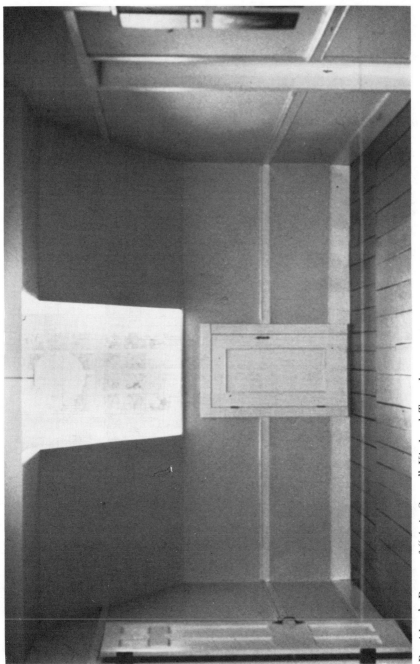

President's Room of "Attic Story," Kirtland Temple

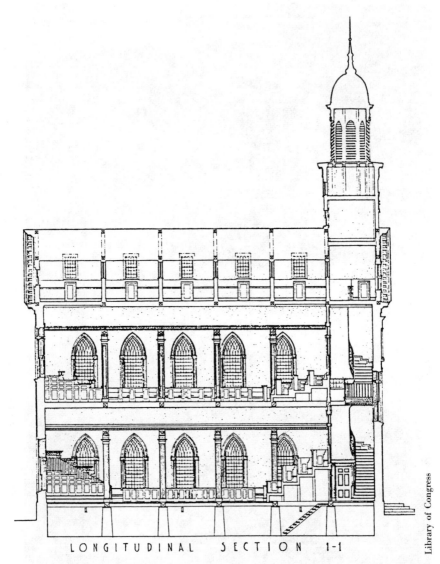

LONGITUDINAL SECTION 1-1

Modern Architectural Drawing of Kirtland Temple

Beman] and prayer by Counselor [Reuben] Hedlock then proceded to anoint the Candadates A[mos] Babcock E[phraim]. Badger S[ampson]. Avard S[olon]. Bragg A[lexander] Cheany I[saac] Perrey Wm Aldrigh Wm W Spencer N[athan]. Cheney J[ohn] Carpenter B[enjamin]. S. Wilber E[dwin]. Web[b] Geo. Dunn L[orenzo]. Snow L[aban]] Mor[r]el

2nd   Names of Elders that united with the quorum I[saac] Decker L[ester]. Brooks

3rd   Coun [John] Morton organized the above Named anointed Elders to call upon the Lord for their Blessings

4th   Pres Beaman Sealed their blessing by Prayer

Names for anointing Next J. Dickson L[ester]. Brooks, W[hitford]. G. Wilson W. W. Willson Elder [Sampson] Avard spoke to the quorum

5th   after Several remark[s] from Different ones the meeting Closed by prayer.

---

[1]The 3rd of April, 1837, was the day appointed for the priesthood brethren to receive their washings and anointings prior to the solemn assembly (see Wilford Woodruff, Journal, under date, Church Archives).

4 April 1837

April 4th 1837

1st   at an adjourned meeting opened by prayer from the president Pres [Alvah] Beaman and Council proseded

the [2nd] Second Botle of oil was Concecreated by pres Beaman Joseph Smith sen & Elder Nickerson

3rd   proseded to anoint Wm Huntington W[hitford]. G. Willson, I[saac] Decker, Geo. C. Willson, L[ester]. Brooks, H[enry]. H. Willson, L[ewis]. D. Willson, B[radley]. B. Willson, W. W. Willson the Councelors wer[e] both anointing Sealed by the president

4   Liberty was given for remarks and Som[e] were made miting Closed by sin[g]ing and prayer

(miting of April 5th is caried forward the other Side of the leafe)

31 March 1837

March 31 1837

the Elders quorum [met] in the Lords house
1st   the meeting opened by the president [Alvah Beman] making remarks and prayer the pres & Coun proseded to ~~anoint~~ consecreate a botle of oile then proseaded to anoint F[reeman]. Nickerson M[oses]. R. Nor[r]iss Richard Breasure H[iram]. Kelogg S[olomon]. Freeman C[ornelius]. P. Lott C[harles]. Wood M[atthew]. Al[l]eon A[bel]. Lamb C[ornelius] G Vanleuven

the above Named Breatheren Joined vocally and Called upon the Lord for the Blessings to rest upon them

the meeting Closed by the presidents Commending the quorum to the most high.

12 April 1837

April 12 1837

1st Meeting opened by prayer from the Clerk
2nd   the pres [Alvah Beman] gave liberty to the Breatheren to make remarks and they improoved it
3rd   Daniel Carter came forward for ordination being in hast[e] to return to his friends in concequenc[e] of both Coun[selors] being absent the pres chose Elders A[bel]. Lamb & M[oses]. R. Noriss pro tem to ordain him
4th   it was moved and Caried that the quorum meet Next We[d]n[e]sday at 1 oclock P. M.

Meeting Closed with prayer.

26 April 1837

April 26 1837

The Elders quorum met in the Lower part of the Lords house Meeting op[e]ned with Sin[g]ing and prayer and liberty was given for remark[s] and Some were made and the meting adjourned by Singing and prayer.

23 July 1837

July 23 1837

The Elders quorum Met in the Lords house op[e]ning pr[a]yer by Coun [Reuben] Hedlock Ex[h]ortation and prayer Elders John Duncan J[ohn]. Pack I[ra]. Willes joined the quorum the meeting closed by prayer.

5 April 1837

April 5 1837

The Elders quorum met in the Lords hous[e] Agreeable to adjournment
1st   op[e]ning prayer by Coun [Reuben] Hedlock
2nd   Coun Hedlock proseaded to ann[o]int the following Breatherin Jeremy Bartlet Chester Jud[d] Nicholas Singley Stephen Reed, Walter M. Blancherd Christopher Stilwell.
3rd   the Breatheren who were anointed prayed for their blesings to to be Sealed upon them
4th   Exortations from Several Breatheren.
5th   the first presidents[1] Came in and Sealed the holy anointing with prayer and the Shout of hosanah

---

[1]Members of the First Presidency.

17 September 1837[1]

[Minutes of a conference of Elders held in the house of the Lord this evening evening   Pres. Joseph Smith Jr Presided. The conferance was op{e}ned by prayer by Pres S{idney}. Rigdon after which the conferance was addressed by the chair on the subject of the gathering of the Saints in the last days and the duties of the of the different quorums relations thereto. It appeared manifest to the conference that the places appointed for the gathering of the Saints were at this time crowded to overflowing & that it was necessary that there be more Stakes of Zion appointed in order that the poor might have a place to gather to. wherefore it was moved seconded & carried by

vote of the whole that Presidents J Smith Jr & S. Rigdon be requested
by this conference to go & appoint other Stakes or places of gathering and that they receive a certificate of this their appointment signed by the Clerk of the Church. Elder William Marks who had been
appointed, in the after part of the day to be the Bishops Agent was
called upon to know if he would accept the appointment he arose
and said that he would comply with the request of the Church & the
Lord being his helper he would discharge the duties thereof to the
best of his abilities. After which the Elders present who were in a
situation to travel were called upon to number themselves, beginning
on the South Side of the house, & to pass to the north. it appeared
that there were one hundred & nine Elders present who wished to
travel. they were then divided into eight companies in the following
manner. Beginning with No 1 to No 12 formed the first company
They were appointed to travel East. The next was from 12 to 26
They were apponted to travel South East. The next was from 26 to 39
They were appointed to travel South. The next from 39 to 52 They
were to travel South west. The next from 52 to 65 They were to go
directly West. The next from 65 to 78 Their course was North west.
The next from 78 to 91 They were to travel North. The next from 91
to 104 They were to travel North East It appeared after this division
that there {were} 5 left Nos 105-6-7-8 and 9 No 105 was appointed
to travel with the company that go South East. 106 with the
Com{pan}y South. 107 to travel with the South Com{pan}y. 108
with the East Company & 109 North. It was farther appointed that
those who might desire to travel a different course from the one
which was appointed to the division to which they belonged, might
have the privilege of Changing with one of another division. And
lastly it was appointed that the different divisions appoint a meeting
for themselves to make such arrangments as they shall think proper
in relation to their journ{e}ying and after prayer by President S.
Rigdon the conference adjourned.

                    G. W. Robinson, Clerk of Church]

------

[1]These minutes are not part of the Elders' Record but are from the Kirtland Council
Minute Book, pp. 243-45. Because of their importance to this document, they have been included here.

24 September 1837

The Elders quorum met in the Lords house
1st   op[e]ning prayer by the first Coun [Reuben] Hedlock
2nd   proposed releife for the Elders to go and preach the gospel
3rd   Elders Joined the quorum A[saph] Blancherd O[liver] Snow J[esse] Baker J[ohn] Pack J[ohn] Lawson.

26 September 1837

The Elders qu[o]rum met in the Lords house
1st   op[e]ning pr[a]yer by coun [John] Morton and Some remarks by the first coun [Reuben] Hedlock.
2nd   petitions for ordainations were called for and the following were persented and ap[p]roved T[ruman] Slyter J[oseph]. Al[l]en E[dwin]. P. Merrium B[enjamin] Kem[p]ton A[bram] Boyington R[ufus] Pack R[euben] Daniels N[ewell]. K. Knight E[leazer] King S[amuel] Frankling   Brother [Isaac] Rogers case was put over to the Next meeting   ten were ordained
3rd   Closing pr[a]yer by the first Coun [Reuben] Hedlock and Dispursed to meet again on the Next Sabbath at 4 o clock

1 October 1837

Oct 1 1837

The Elders quorum met in the Lords house
1st   meeting op[e]ned by prayer and proseded to buisness
2nd   proseded to Examin Recommends for ordaination and the following Names were unanamously received Anson Cull [Call] Wm Carter Harvey Strong A[a]ron Johnson Lusus N. Scovil Isaac Clevland Reuben Fields, Isaac Rogers, Isaac Huburd [Hubbard].
3rd   Meeting adjourned with prayer

8 October 1837

Oct 8 1837

The quorum of Elders met in the Lords house
1st   op[e]ning pray[er] by first councilor [Reuben Hedlock]

2nd   proseaded to ordain the following breatherin Anson Call,
Wm Carter H[arvey] Strong A[aron] Johnson L[ucius]. N. Scovil
I[saac] Cleavland R[euben] Fields I[saac]. Rogers I[saac] Hubbard
3rd   Meeting adjourned with prayer

15 October 1837

Oct 15 1837

The Elders quorum met in the Lords house
1st   op[e]ning ad[d]ress and prayer by the president [Alvah
Beman]
2nd   proseaded to No[.] the Elders to know which way they would
go to preach
3rd   the quorum voted to keep the word of wisdom[1] and all the
Commandments
4th   Thomas Curtis was ordained meeting adjourned by prayer

---

[1]The Word of Wisdom—Section 89 of the *Doctrine and Covenants*—as given in the spring of 1833 commanded that the Saints totally abstain from the use of alcohol, tobacco, and hot drinks (tea and coffee). However, because of wide-spread use of and deep-seated attachment to these substances by members, this revelation, by 1834, was changed from a direct commandment to general advise only. Even so, zealous leaders and members pressed for compliance with the original meaning of the revelation, and in early December 1836, a unanimous vote of the Saints in Kirtland supported the complete abstenance of "all liquors from the Church in Sickness & in health except wine at the Sacraments & for external washing" (Wilford Woodruff, Journal, 4 December 1836).

22 October 1837

Oct 22 1837

   The quorum of Elders met in the Lords house
1st   the op[e]ning prayer by pres Joseph Smith Sen
2nd   the following Canadates were called and ordained Stephen
Hedlock Warren Smith John Hammond Hiram Bennis[1] Michal
Umans Arnold He[a]ly, Orren Cheney
Meeting adjourned with singing and prayer

---

   [1]This name cannot be positively deciphered. The last name could be "Bemis" or "Berris".

29 October 1837

Oct 29 1837

The Elders quorum met in the Lords house

1st   Opened by Singing and prayer   motioned by Elder [Reuben] Hedlock and Caried by unanamous vote that all the Elders that traveled to preach Should observe and teach the Word of wisdom to others or be reported to ~~this~~ the Elders quorum and their Licence be Demanded.[1]

2nd   Joel Harvey was ordained an Elder Henry Stephens was ordained a priest

3rd   voted that we me[e]t on We[d]n[e]sday afternoon untill Diferent arang[e]ments were made

---

[1]Note how serious the Kirtland Elders' Quorum was regarding the Word of Wisdom.

1 November 1837

Nov 1st 1837

The Elders quorum met in the Lords house

1st   op[e]ning pr[a]yer by Elder [Reuben] Hedlock.

2nd   David Dixon was ordained a priest and Samuel Parker Was ordained an Elder   meeting Closed by pr[a]yer by S[tephen]. Hedlock.

15 November 1837

Nov 15 1837

The Elders quorum met in the Lords house

1st   opening prayer by Coun [Reuben] Hedlock

A prayer put up for pres [Alvah] Beaman   the Name of Brother Ha[y]se was Called for ordaination and Disaproved by the quorum

2nd   Wm Earls was recommended before the quorum for the office of an Elder   aproved by the quorum and ordained

3rd   Luke Luckone was recomme[n]ded before the quorum for the office of a priest   a[p]proved by the quorum and ordained

4th   the Diffeculti betw[e]en Elder [Reuben] Fields and Elder

[Samuel] Franklin was Brought before the quorum and Laid open till the next meeting   Closed by prayer to meet Wendsday Next.

23 November 1837

Nov 23 1837

The Elders quorum met in the Lords house
1st   op[e]ning prayer by Elder [John] Morton
2nd   the Dificulte between E[lder]. Reubin Fields and E[lder]. Samuel Franklin was brought before the quorum and Sset[t]led Satisfactorley and Shook Hands in token of fellowship
3rd   Br Charles Bird recomen[d]ed for ordaination   vote Called & caried unanamously   meting Closed by prayer by E[lder] [Reuben] Hedlock

27 November 1837[1]

[A Conference of Elders constituting of all the authorities of the Church of Latter Day Saints; convened in the Lords House in Kirtland for the purpose of electing & ordaining a president to preside over the quorum of Elders, in the place of Elder {Alvah} Beman Diseased.[2]

Pres. Joseph Smith Sen. (who presided) then Nominated Elder Ruben Hadlock. Elder Hadlock was seconded and elected by a unanymous voice of the conference. The Pres. then chose Elder B[righam]. Young & Asael Smith to assist him in ordaining Elder Hadlock to this office. After prayer conf{erence} adjourned.

G. W. Robinson Clerk & record]

---

[1]These minutes are not part of the Elders' Record but are from the "Kirtland Council Minute Book," p. 265. However, because of their relevance to this document, they have been included here.

[2]Alvah Beman died about the 20th of November, 1837.

29 November 1837

Nov the 29 1837

The quorum of Elders met in the Lords house
1st   op[e]ning prayer by the pres [Reuben Hedlock] and Some

prelimenary remarks

2nd   Edmond Bosley ordained 2nd Counselor

3rd   Edward Thomson presented before the quorum for ordaination   Caried for ordaination by unanmous vote

4th   Stephen Perrey was persented before the quorum and received
the San[c]ttion of the quorum for the of[f]ice of a priest

5th   the charge that was perfered before the quorum against Elder
Sollomon Freeman by William Perry for the crime of polygamy was
brought forward.[1] Elder Freeman plead not gilty of the charge[.]
[T]estimony for the Complainant came forward (Dexter Stilman) and
Stated that Elder Freeman had a wife in Tollan township Co of
Berksheir in Mass, and it was told him there that he (E. Freeman)
Came a way [without his][2] wife   Elder Harlow Redfield Stated that
when he and Elder Stilman went to See Elder Freeman. Elder
Freeman ackno[w]loged that he come away and left his wife as was
testified   Elder Freeman ackno[w]loged before the quorum that he
had left his first wife came away with and Soon Commenced living
with another woman he further Stated he did not know but his first
wife was yet living   he further Stated he would not go acros the
room to obtain a bill from her   Elder Freeman Manifest a
Car[e]less indifferent spirit

6th   Wm F. Huntington was presented before the quorum for ordination   he viewed the aprobation of the quorum for the office of
a priest

last   Closed by prayer from the president

---

[1]Although the Prophet Joseph Smith (and, perhaps, Oliver Cowdery,) had earlier
entered into the practice of plural marriage in Kirtland, the Church officially condemned
polygamous relationships (see *Doctrine and Covenants of the Church of the Latter Day
Saints* (Kirtland: 1835), Section 101, p. 251).

[2]The bracketed words indicate the probable wording although the original here is too
faint to read.

6 December 1837

December 6th 1837

1   The Elders met according to Appointment Meeting opened by
Prayer By President [Reuben] Hedlock After a few Prelimenary
Remarks by the President

2   Proceeded to Buisness the Case of Brother M[ichael]. Unans

Brought before the quorum but put over in conciquience of the absence of the Parties

3   Brother Alexander Wright was Recomended to the Quorum of Priests for Ordernation

4   Brother Charles Bird received Ord[i]nation from ~~The~~ under the hands of the President and the 1th Couns[e]lor

5   Some Appropriations Made for Paper in order to help on the Publication of the Elders Journal[1]

---

[1]Two issues of the *Elders' Journal* (October and November 1837) were printed in Kirtland, Ohio. Joseph Smith was editor and Thomas B. Marsh was publisher.

13 December 1837

Dec 13 1837

The Elders quorum met in the Lords house

1st   op[e]ning prayer by Coun [Edmund] Bosley   the quorum proseded to speak their fealings to each other

2nd   the Case of Brother Michal Umans was brought before the quorum the pla[i]ntiff being present the Statement was made before the quorum   the trial was adjourned untill Br Umans Returned home from his Mission

3rd   Reseved some money to assist in procurin[g] paper for the Elders Journal Closing prayer by the president

31 December 1837

Dec 31 1837

At my house[1] ordain[ed] Br Asa Bills

---

[1]Because he was the clerk, perhaps this refers to the home of Evan M. Greene.

3 January 1838

Jan 3d 1838

The Elders met accord[i]ng to adjourment in the house of the Lord. Meeting opened by prayer quoram voted to number themselves for the purpose of speaking in the quoram during the winter by turns. quoram also voted to meet on Monday eavning instead of Wednesday eavnings as a quoram in the house of the Lord, during the winter, voted that 20 minnets be aloted to each one to speak; and that six speak in an eavning meeting adjourned untill Monday eavning by prayer

Alex[ande]r Cheney {scribe

8 January 1838

Monday eavning, Jan 8th 1838

The Elders met according [to] adjournment. Meeting opened by prayer. Six of the first number were called on to declaim[1] adjourn till next Monday eavning

A[lexander]. Cheney {Scribe

---

[1]To make a formal speech or oration.

15 January 1838

Monday eavning Jan 15th 1838

The Elders met according to adjournment. Meeting open by prayer. quoram proceded to make some rules, by which they should be governed in regard to their speaking in the quoram: Voted that the six might occupy the time aloted them (i.e.) if the first Elder did not choose to occupy his 20 minnets, the second might speak, during the remainder of the first Elder's 20 minnets, as well as the 20 minnets aloted to himself, and so on to the sixth speaker.

Voted also, that if the numbers called in regular rotation were not there, they would loose their privolege of speaking of until their turn came around again, six Elders were called to speak: the Elders presant, who had not been presant before, numbered themselves to speak in ther turn   Meeting closed by prayer

A[lexander] C[heney]: {Scribe

January 1837

[Illegible number] January
Reckord[ed] over the leaf[1]

---

[1]Clerk's note that the rest of the minutes for January 1837 were recorded on the next page.

8 February 1837

The Elders Met Feb 8 1837   Being duly org[a]nized the meeting was opened by prayer   names of Elders Recvd E F Waller[?]
Names for Ordination David Fulmer James S Holman Rufus Pack Closed with prayer

10 February 1837

Reference to page 22[1]

Elders Met Feby 10   The Pres [Alvah Beman] Addressed the quorum Concerning faithfullness   the Bretheren renued thair Covenant   the Committee[2] reported they had seen Elder S[amuel]. Canfield he replied he had nothing against the quorum but distance which he Lived from the Lords House was the Reason of his not attending the meetings but had not seen Elders S[tarry]. Fisk and W[illiam]. Barker to Labour with them

Closed by prayer

---

[1] This is the clerk's note that these minutes for the year 1837 would fit chronologically at page 22 of the original record.

[2] Apparently an ad hoc committee of elders assigned to labor with wayward or inactive members of the quorum.

17 February 1837

Elders quorum met in the Lords House Feb 17 1837
Opened by Prayer   Pres [Alvah] Beman made some remark[s] on the subject of a Vigilence Committee[1] consisting of three Elders: to this Office Elders P[eter] Shirts A[bel] Lamb and Joshua Holman were appointed   Moved and Caried that the names of the Elders be read at the next meeting   Names of Elders Recd Martin Titus Joseph Cooper   meeting closed with Singing

---

[1] A standing committee of three elders to stay watchful or alert to improprieties or irregularities among members of the quorum.

22 February 1837

Feb 22

The Elders quorum met in the Lords house
1th   Meeting opened by prayer
2nd   Brother [David] Fulmores case was presented for Ordination   he was a going to return could not wait untill the Council Set
therefore his case was laid before the quorum   Pres [Alvah] Beaman
called for a vote and which was in the affirmative
2   Proceded to ordain D[avid] Fulmer and Coun [Reuben] Hedlock
spoke
3   the Clerk [Evan M. Greene] Read the names of the Elders
adjourned by Prayer

22 January 1838

Kirtland Jan 22nd 1838

The Elders met, in the house of the Lord. Meeting opened by
prayer.   six, according to the before apointmen[t] and regulation,
declaimed. Pres. [Reuben] Hadlock informed the quoram that their
clerk, Elder Evan M. Green, had moved away from Kirtland,
therefore it was necessary to elect an other Clerk in his place: Alexander Cheney was elected, to be the clerk of the Elderss quoram. Prs
Hadlock and council, P[ro] T[em] ordained Samuel Fowler, Rodman
Clark, and Amos Jackson, to be Elders. Meeting closed by prayer
A[lexander]. C[heney]. Clk

29 January 1838

Jan 29th 1838

The Elders met, as usual, meeting opened by singing, and prayer.
six Elders declaimed. Prs [Reuben] Hadlock and his Council, P[ro].
T[em]. orda[i]ned Lewis Eager, Erastus Babbit, and Martin H. Peck,
to be Elders. Meeting closed by prayer
A[lexander]. C[heney]. Clk

5 February 1838

Feb 5th 1838

The Elders met. Metting open by prayer. the six, who were pre-sant of the numbers between 47 & 56[1] inclusive declaimed. Prs. Had[l]ock made some preliminary remarks, and then read the revela-tion given to Thomas B. Marsh July 23d 1837.[2] Closed by prayer

A[lexander]. C[heney]. Clk

---

[1]Ninety-six elders formed a quorum, and for purposes of "declaiming," each had been assigned a number.

[2]D&C 112.

26 February 1838

Kirtland Feb 26th 1838.

The Elders met in the house of the Lord.
Meeting was opened by singing & prayer
Warren Smith was elected Clerk. The former one [Alexander Cheney] had moved away. Pres [Reuben] Hadlock made some remarks Con-cerning moveing to Zion.[1] and then preceded to appoint a Councillor Martin H Peck was ordained under the hand of pres Hadlock to that office. a vote was called and carried that no one should have a letter of recommendation to go to Zion[2] unless they kept the word of wisdom. after many remarks being made on diferents subjects The pres proceded to ordain Thomas B. Fisher, John Lamoreaux Wm Mc-Clary Elders.

Warren Smith. Clerk

---

[1]At this time "Zion" meant Far West, Missouri, and vicinity.

[2]Three elders or a bishop needed to sign a recommendation to move to Missouri (see D&C 72:25).

6 March 1838

March 6th 1838. The Elders quorum met in the House of the Lord. meeting was opened by Councillor [Martin] H. Peck by singing and prayer there not being any buisness of importance to transact the time was spent in exhorting singing & prayer

W[arren]. Smith Clerk

12 March 1838

March 12th 1838

The Elders met as usu[a]l in the hous[e] of the Lord in the at[t]ic Story meeting was open[e]d by bro [John] Morton by singing and prayre bro [John] Grible mad[e] application for an ordination and it was thought best that he Should apply unto the Lesser priests quorum for an ordination. bro brown[1] arose and desiered that hands then should be laid on him for a re[s]teration of his health another brother requested a reccommend as he was a going to preach & did not expect to return until the quorum was gone to the west bro Morton told him his License[2] would be the best reccommend that he could have

W[arren]. Smith Clerk

---

[1] Albert or Benjamin Brown.

[2] After being ordained to the office of elder and receiving a certificate to that effect, a male priesthood holder could apply for an elder's license to preach the gospel and perform other appropriate priesthood duties.

26 March 1838

March 26th 1838

The Elders quorum [met] in the Lords House meeting opened by bro [Martin] Peck by prayer. A charge was then prefered against bro John Gribble by J[ohn]. Sawyer & L[uman]. Carter stating that he had gone and rec[e]iv[e]d, an ordination in the Elders quorum without magnifiing his calling in the Priest quorum agreable to his covenant. A vote was called and carried that the case should be transfered to the high Council.

W[arren]. S[mith]. Clk.

31 March 1838

March 31st 1838

The Elders qu[o]rum met in the Lords house   bro [Martin] Peck opened the meeting by prayer & then gave leave for remarks, accordingly the meeting was carried on by exortation prayer & singing &c.   W[arren]. S[mith]. Clk.

7 April 1838

April 7th 1838. The Elders met in the Lords House as usual meeting opened by bro [Martin] Peck by Calling on the Lord in prey[e]r after some remarks had been made by different brethren bro L[orenzo]. Wells prefered a charged against bro Amos Babcock   s[ai]d case was a[d]journed for one week   meeting closed by asking the Lord to bless the quorum.

W[arren]. S[mith]. Clk.

14 April 1838

April 14th 1838.   Elders met as usual   meeting opened by bro [John] Morton by singing and pray[e]r   the case of bro [Lorenzo] Wells and [Amos] Babcock was then brought up after reading the charge which read as follows, br B[abcock]. accused bro W[ells] of stealing or taking that which was not his own and his wife of tatling lying & mischief making and said he could prove the same   they proceeded to examin[e] ~~which~~ witnesses which testified in favor of Wells   the quorum decided that bro Bab[cock] should confess to bro Wells and make the plaster as broad as the sore the meeting broke up in in Order with prayer

W[arren]. S[mith]. Clk

21 April 1838

April 21st 1838.

The Elders quorum met in the Lords House meeting opened by singing & by Pre[s]. [Reuben] Hadlock caling on the Lord in prayer after Pre[s] Hadlock and some others had made some remarkes the case of br Babcock was called up after a few remarks had been made by a number of the brethren br Bab[cock] was called on to speak his mind & make confession if he saw fit he did make some confession Pre[s] Hadlock then called a vote of the quorum to know if they were satisfied with the confession

the quorum voted sattisfied

W[arren]. S[mith]. Clk

28 April 1838

April 28th

The quorum of Elders met as usual in the Lords house meeting opened by W[arren] Smith by singing and pray[e]r meeting carried on by Exhortation and pray[e]r   one bro came forward to have hands laid on him for his   health meeting closed by pray[e]r

W[arren] Smith Clk

3 May 1838

May 3d 1838.   The Elders met as usual.   Meeting opened by singing and prayer by W[arren]. Smith   Pres [Reuben] Hadlock came in directly and enquired if there was any buisness before the quoram bro Andrew Lamoreaux arose and said he was grieved on account of the conduct [of] bro Joshua Bosley he says he found him drunk and a short time after he conversed with him and he confessed and hoped he ~~she~~ should not do the like again but has been found under the same transgression again it was then agreed that three or four of the brethren should go and convers[e] with him and see how he felt

W[arren]. Smith Clk

20 May 1838

Kirtland May 20th 1838.   The Elders quorum met Sunday morning at eight oclock in the at[t]ic Story of the Lords house
meeting opened by preyer by Pres [Reuben] Hadlock Clark Draper [was] ordained Elder   W[arren] Smith, Clk

3 June 1838

June 3rd 1838

The Elders quorum met at the house of Elder [Reuben] Hedlocks op[e]ning prayer by the president
The Case of Elder Joshua Bosley was brought before the quorum and it being proved that he was then actualy intoxacated and had broken his covena[n]t he made with the quorum[1] the hand of fellowship was with Drawn from him the Situation of the quorum was taken in to consideration and was Laid over untill next meeting Br Parker was reccomended by Wm Marks to the office of a priest a vote was taken that he Should receive that office

---

[1]Members of the Kirtland Elders' Quorum had covenanted to keep the "Word of Wisdom" as per the vote of the Church in Kirtland 4 December 1836. See minutes for 15 and 29 October 1837.

10 June 1838

June 10 1838

The Elders Quorum Met Sunday P. M. 4 Oclock In the Attic Story of the Lords House
Meeting Op[e]ned by counselor [John] Morton by Prayer   after some Remarks by the President [Reuben Hedlock] on the subject of his Leaving hear for the Far West1 that some one Must be Chosen to fill the Vacancy Accordingly He recommended Counselor Morton to fill the Vacancy as it is his priviliage as first Counselor to the Presidency of this Quorum   President [William] Marks Made some remarks that Elder Mortons Abilities and understanding the buisness of the Quorum qu[a]llified him for this office In Prefferance to Any other one And had the sperit of prophecy to that affect that Elder Morton should hold the office of Prisedent of this Quorum   Bishop [Newel K.] Whitney allso made Some Remarkes to the propriety of Councelor Mortons being choosing to fill this office as it was his priviliage to go forward and not back as It belong to him from the Concideration of his filling the office of First Councelor In the Presedency of this Quorum These remark came In Consequence of Counselor Mortons Declining or wishing some other to be choosing in his place saying he would Act as Counselor or was willing to be a

priviate member of the Quorum Elder [Hiram] Kellogg President
of the high priests Quorum spake and said he had been Acquainted
with Elder Morton this many years and since he had been in
Kirtland had formed more particualer acquantance as once Belonging to the Quorum of Elders and It was his wishes that Counselor
Morton Receive the Ordination of Prisedent of the Elders

1   Voted that Elder Morton Be ordained President of the Elders
Quorum

2   Voted that the Next Sabbath be the time of Ordenation

3   Closed by prayer

---

[1]In the spring of 1838, Far West, Caldwell County, Missouri, became the gathering
place of the Church. Hundreds of Latter-day Saints residing in Kirtland and vicinity
emigrated to Missouri at that time.

17 June 1838

June 17 1838

This day Quorum of Elders Met at the Lords   House The
Meeting Opened by Prayer   after some remarks Proceeded to the Or-
dination of Counselor Morton To the office of President over the
Elders Quorum Hands was laid on by President [William] Marks
Bishop [Newel K.] Whitney President [Hiram] Kellogg [and] Presi-
dent Hadlock

1th   Prayer by President Marks and Procceded to Ordination

2   Closed by Singing after a few remarks

3   and Prayer

24 June 1838

June 24th 1838

The Elders Quorum Met in the Lords House   After Prayer by
President [John] Morton Proceeded

1   Is thair any Buisness before the Quorum Ans[wer] (none) as thair
was no buisness to attend too the meeting was opened for Prayer exhortation or to Express thair feelings as the sperit may direct. It was
a time of Refreshing to many as the Lord was in our Midst By his
spirit

2   Closed by Prayer by Brother [Martin] Peck

1 July 1838

July 1

The Elders Quorum Met in the Lords House After prayer by the President [John Morton] Proceeded to buisness after some few remarkes it was proposed that this meeting Be a meeting of inquirey as to the state of feeling and Each to express thair feelings as the spirit shall direct   It was a good and profitiable meeting all manefest a spirit of union and peace as becometh Saints of god

8 July 1838

July 8th

The Elders Quorum Met according to appointment and being duly Organized Proceeded first by Prayer by Elder [Hezekiah] Fisk and

1   then confered freely on the the subject and interist of this Quorum and best interiest of the cause of our Redeemer
2   The President [John Morton] Proceeded in the Ordination of H[ezekiah]. Fisk as 1st counselor and then Proceeded in the Ordination of L[ahasa] Hollister as 2nd Counselor   May the sperrit of Elijah[s] God inspire them with true wisdom that they may Counsol in all Ritcheousness and hevenly wisdom shewing themselves to be treuly men of god in all things   after few remarks Adjourned by prayer by Counsolor Hollester.

15 July 1838

July 15 1838

The Elders Quro Quorum Met in the Lords House   After Prayer by Counselor [Lehasa] Hollester Proceeded to buisness   six names was presented for Ordination (Viz) William Shoeman Henry Moore Charles Green Jeremiah Knights thair abilities and moral standing and [a]bout to take a vote to receiving of them to Ordination brother [Willard] Woodstock High priest   Brother [John] Sawyer a Priest object to thair Ordination on the Account of thair not passing through the Lessor Priesthood as they concidered proper and necesery[1]   After some Arguments for and against such Procedings a motion was made to refer to counsel of the Church accordingly Voted that a counsel of the authorieties of the church be cauled to meet in the Lords house Satuarday next at 1 Oclock to take this subject in concideration Moti[o]ened we adjourn this meeting   Closed by Prayer by Brother Woodstock

---

[1]The need for an adult male member to prove himself as an Aaronic Priesthood holder before being ordained to the Melchizedek Priesthood, was starting to be viewed as a necessary practice. However, this was not then official policy nor was it instituted at this time.

22 July 1838

July 22

The Elders Quorum Met in the Lords House   Meeting opened by Prayer   Proceeded to Buisness.   Voted that Justus Blood Jeremiah Knight   Charles Green   John Pulsipher   Oliver Wetherby   Henry Marsden be received in this Quorum By Ordination   Accordingly proceeded in the Laying on of hands By President [John] Morton and with his Counselors H[ezekiah] Fisk and L[ahasa] Hollister with the Assistance of ~~Br~~ Counselor Cole[1] and Counselor [Hiram] Kellogg of the Presidency of the Church in which the above Brethering ware duely ordained with the exception of Brother Pulsipher who was Absent   Charge by Presd. [John] Morton Meeting Adjourned by Prayer by Coun. Kellogg

---

[1]Perhaps Zerah S. Cole.

29 July 1838

July 29 1838

The Elders Quorum Met in the Lords House   Meeting Opened by Prayer by Counr. [Lehasa] Hollister. Proceeded to the Ordination of J[ohn] A[c]kerly [and] H[enry] Moore Hands was laid on By Pres [John] Morton & his Couns. H[ezekiah] Fisk [and] L Hollister Brother W[illiam] Shoeman was rejected for the want of a Christian Chari[c]ter Brother Boyce was recommended to the priest Quorum for Ordination Closed by Prayer

5 August 1838

July August 5

The Elders Quorum Met in the Lords House   Prayer by Presd. [John] Morton   As there was no buisness before the Quorum the time was taken up in Prayer and Exhortation to the edification and Blessing of the whole Adjourned by prayer

12 August 1838

August 12

The Elders Quorum Met in the Lords House   the Meeting Opened by prayer and then proceeded to buisness   Jessee Montgomery was received to Ordination by a an unamamous vote   proceeded to the Laying on of hands by Pres [John] Morton and his Counselors H[ezekiah] Fisk and L[ahasa] Holister and Co[u]ncelor [Hiram] Kellogg and Elder [Noah] Packerd   Adjourned by Prayer

19 August 1838

August 19

The Elders Quorum met in the Lords House   the meeting Opened by prayer as there was no buisness brought before the Quorum the time was taking up by prayer and exhortation or the expressing of thare needs as the spirit should dictate   Pres [John] Morton propose that the Quorum take up some subject for discusion Justus Blood prop[o]se that we speak from this subject   is the Comforter Christ promised to send the Holy Ghost   is the Holy Spirit the Holy Ghost   How the Different Denominations have the Holy sperit or the Holy Ghost among them   do they know anything of its opperation and affects   proposed that this be the subject of discusion the next Meeting

26 August 1838[1]

August 26

Elders Met in the Lords House   the above subject was brought before the meeting that each one might speak without refferance to any one opinion upon this subject and express his v[i]ews   The whole Quroum had an Oppo[r]tunity each one   they most all freely spoke and gave frankly there feelings on this subject   They ware a great [agreed] in opinion that the Holy Spirit was the Holy Ghost or the comforter that Christ promised to send but his peiple or the saints of god might so live that they may not injoye but a little or they may live so near as to keep all the commandments of God and injoye a fullness of the spirit that proceeds from the Father and the son which fullness is the Holy Ghost that they may prophesey and speak in tongues and give the inturpertation of Tongues   and farther that the sectarains do not have the Holy Ghost but injoye a measure of the spirit as a light to inlighting thare understanding that they may see and obey the gospell that they might injoye or receive the fullness even the Holy Ghost   Elder [Noah] Packard said he did not think that anyone Had the Holy Spirit or knew of its opperations but those who obey the gospel through the testamoney of his servents whome god has sent in preaching repentance through faith and baptisim for remission of sins and the Laying on of hands for the reseption of the Holy Ghost   He thought that no people Preast or people knew anything a bought the Holy Spirit but was lead or had a Spirit which was the spirit of the Devil.   After Prayer we adjourned to meet again upon the same subject

---

[1]The fact that there are not additional minutes for the year 1838 (nor for 1839) attests to the general disruption of Church activities in Kirtland caused by apostasy and the subsequent departure of most of the Saints to Missouri.

13 March 1840

Quorum met agreeable to appointment at the house of Amos Babcock on the 13th of March 1840 for the purpose of trying Brother Charles Wood for improper conduct to a Sister Shumon   brother John Morton Presided The charges prefered were 1st For improper conversation and conduct toward her   2nd for making a proposal to go to her house if she would sleep with him   3d putting his arm a round her neck in a Lewd and improper manner and offering abuse by saying many woman get their living that way   4th trying to get her on the bed with him   the above charges were made out against him   voted his Licence be taken from him and withheld untill he make satisfaction by confession to the Church   John Gaylord Clerk protem

18 October 1840

Oct 18 1840

Quorum Met. Meeting opened by prayer   the Case of Henry Moore came up by a complaint entered by Amos Babcock that he the said Henry had manifest an unnatural and unchristian like conduct to towards his wife in striking her in anger— 2nd for denying the above facts and pronouncing it to be a lie without the least foundation of truth— 3d for illtreatment to brother Brown in refusing to pay him an honest demand   4 for unwise conduct not approbated by the Elders of the church
The first and second charges he was acquited   the 3d [was] inpart made out against him and agrees to pay Brother Brown as soon as he can get means and he was acquitted
A charge prefered against John Norton by Henry Fosmire for retaining property that was not his own to the injurey of the said Fosmire   2nd for unchristian treatment to me when Labouring for a reconciliation for the above treatment   The above charge was not proved to the satisfaction of the Quorum conciquently Elder Norton was discharged provided he would suffer the said Fosmire to enter the primisses and to take of the property he had bought of Amadon

22 October 1840

Oct 22 1840

Quorum Met pursuant to adjournment in the house of the Lord for the purpose of taking into concideration the case of Elder Henry Moore in the following charges prefered by Elder Charles Thompson Viz   1sth   Prophecying false in the name of the Lord
2nd   Trying to persuade a woman to promise to have him while his own wife is still living
3d   Trying to persuade her to covenent with him to pray that his wife might die

4th   Telling her (she being a widow) that if she ever marries any other man than him She should not come forth in the first Resurection when he had every reason to believe his wife was yet living

5th   Lying and deception

6th   pronouncing curses upon Elder Charles Thompson because he would not uphold him in the above abominations and washing his feet against me for the same reason

7th   Lazyness and leaving his family to suffer

Henry Moore was duely notified of this meeting but refusing to attend a motion was made and secon[d]ed that we withdraw fellowship from him and his Licence be required of him   accordingly a vote was taken and he was cut off from this Quorum

No Date

Met in the Lords house   the case of David C Draper came up wherein he stood charged with drunkness and deception and want of wisdom to magnify his calling as an Elder   to the several charges he pled not guilty untill proven but his previous conduct being so bad a motion was made to withdraw fellowship from him that he no longer be a member of this Quorum   accordingly a vote was taken and he was cut of[f]

11 November 1840

November 11th 1840

The Elders Quorum meet in the House of the Lord and President Morton informed the Quorum that he had been ordained in to the high Priest Quorum. The Quorum proceded to elect Amos Babcock President and Otis Hobart and Thomas Green Councilors and Otis Hobart clerk

24 December 1840

December 24th

Quorum met persuant to adjournment and took in to consideration a charge preferd against Elder Thomas Dutcher by Samuel

Phelps and Harrison Burges for preaching Doctrine that was not approved of by this Church and for nourishing an inthu[s]eastic spirit
Brother Dutcher was a[c]quitted   Otis Hobart Clerk

8 January 1841

January 8th 1841

The Elders Quorum meet.   meetting opened by prayer   A
charge prefered by Hyrum Kellogg against Lehasa Hollister for saying that he was accessory to ~~stealing~~ taking window sash that did not
belong to him Brother Kellogg sustained his charge
O[tis]. Hobart Clerk

15 January 1841

January 15th 1841

Quorum met in the house of the Lord   Brother [Lehasa] Hollister
moved for a rehearing and it was granted   Desision was made that
Brother Hollister had said that Brother [Hiram] Kellogg was accessory to ~~stealing~~ taking window sash that did not belong to him
Brother Hollister sustained his charge   Brother Kellogg then giv[e]
notice that he should apeal the case to higher authority   accordingly
it was done
O[tis]. Hobart Clerk
A charge preferd against Elder John Cooley By H. Kellogg for refusing to giv[e] up his stove and pipe   Brother Cooley made confession
and Was forgiven
O[tis]. H[obart]. Clerk

10 February 1841

Febuary 10th 1841

The Quorum met in the House of The Lord   meetting opened by
prayer   A charge was prefer[e]d against Elder Hilan Davis by Otis
Hobart for abusing and refusing to liv[e] with His Wife   Brother
Davis was found guilty   the hand of fellowship was with Drawn
from him and his Licence was given up   O[tis]. H[obart]. Clerk

1 March 1841

March 1th 1841

The Elders Quorum met in the Lords House   meetting opened by prayer   Brother Hyland Davis come before the meetting and made confession and on the sabbath following went before the congregation and made his acknowledgement and was forgiven and the hand of fellowship was restored and he received his licence given to him again by the clerk   O[tis]. H[obart]. Clerk

March 1841

March 1841

A charge preferd against Elder Ira Fisk by Brother Henry Moore for saying that he was a liar and he could prove it   the Quorum proceeded to try said case   Brother Fisk acknoweledge the assertion then proceeded and prooved the same   Brother Moore then appeald the case to higher Authority and accordingly it was done
O[tis]. H[obart]. (Clerk)

21 March 1841

March 21th 1841

The Elders quorum met in the Lords House and in consequence of some of the members of the quorum having absented themselves for a long time a committy was appointed to visit the Brethering Brother [William] McClarry and Brother Chapman was appointed for that purpose   the remainder of the time was spent By President [Amos] Babcock and others in exortation   the spirit of the Lord was evidently with the Brethering
O[tis]. H[obart]. (Clerk)

28 March 1841

March 28th 1841

Acording to appointment the quorum met in the attick story of the Lords House   Brother [William] McClary and Chapman that was previously appointed ware presant and reported   President [Amos] Babcock then presented the wishes of Brother [Oliver] Granger to the quorum on the subject of the Hous[e] of the Lord and desired an expresion w[h]ether they ware willing for the House to be used for the purpose of exhibitions as he held the keys   the subject was taken up and it was consider[e]d that as the church was organized according to law and Trustees being appointed[1] and the Keys once being Deliverd to them the quorum voted that the controle of the house belong to the Trustees and it was unanimousley voted that Brother Granger be requested to deliver up the keys to the trustee that he received them from viz Brother H[iram]. Winter[s]   Brother [Otis] Hobart was chosen to inform Brother Granger of the procedings of the meeting   meetting closed by prayre and dismist

O[tis]. H[obart]. Clerk

---

[1]On the 30th of January, 1841, Joseph Smith became Trustee-in-Trust for the Church of Jesus Christ of Latter-day Saints in Illinois. Similarly, the Church was legally organized in Ohio at this time with functioning trustees. Note how the meetings of the Kirtland Elders' Quorum became the forum for handling general Church matters. This quorum was virtually the only organized, functioning priesthood quorum in Kirtland and consequently exercised broad administrative powers.

4 April 1841

April 4th 1841

The Elders Quorum met in the Lords House according to appointment   Bro [Otis] Hobart Reported to the quorum that Brother [Oliver] Granger refused to giv[e] up the Keys of the Lords Hous[e] to the Trustees and sent a letter to be read before the quorum from Brother Joseph Smith on the subject of his holding the Keys[1]   the letter was read by the clerk   the Brethering was still of the opinion that the Trustees ought to hold the Keys and further more it was agreed to let the subject rest at present where it was. Brother Knap[2] was appointed to see and request Brother [David] C. Draper to meet with the quorum at their next meetting and Bro Chapman and Bro Knap to visit Bro [Ira] Bond and request him to meet with the Brethering at their next meetting   voted that Bro [William] McClary should hav[e] his Licenc[e] renewed

O[tis]. H[obart]. Cl[erk]

[1]See Joseph Smith to Oliver Granger, 26 January 1841, cited in Jessee, *Writings of Joseph Smith*, pp. 489-91: "I am pleased you have secured the keys of the Lords House, and should advise you and you are hereby requested to hold them until [I] come." Again on the 4th of May, 1841, the Prophet enjoined Granger to "keep possession of the Keys of the House of the Lord until you receive further instructions from me" (Joseph Smith to Oliver Granger, 4 May 1841, cited in ibid., pp. 494-95). Oliver Granger was appointed as president of the Church in Kirtland by the Prophet in early 1840 (see Joseph Smith to Granger, July 1840, cited in ibid., p. 477), but in October of that year Almon Babbitt was named to asssume that office since it was believed that Granger was returning to Nauvoo. Granger did not move west and this obviously created some bad feelings among these brethren and the Saints in Ohio. For a brief period Babbitt did serve as the presiding leader of the Church in Kirtland; Granger, nevertheless, retained control of the temple. See 12 September 1841, note 1.

[2]Perhaps John Knapp.

11 April 1841

April 11th 1841

The Elders quorum met in the House of the Lord   meetting opened by prayer   Brother Faulk was presented for ordination   his case was taken up and President [Amos] Babcock and Brother [Otis] Hobart and [John] Norton proceded to ordain him to the office of an Elder

O[tis]. H[obart]. Clerk

25 April 1841

April 25th 1841

The quorum of Elders met in the attick story of the Lords House   the case of Brother J[ohn]. Lamoraux was presented to the quorum for ordination   it was voted that he should be ordained to the office of an Elder   the President [Amos Babcock] with others proceded and ordained him

O[tis] H[obart]. Clerk

11 May 1841

May 11th 1841

The Elders quorum met in the House of the Lord   A charge was prefer[e]d a gainst Elder John Lamoreaux for unchristian conduct manifested to different females by F[leullen]. Knapp   the case was taken up and tried   the right hand of fellowship was with drawn and he had untill the next sabbath to make restitution. the quorum met on the following sabbath   Brother Lamoreaux came forward and made his confession the hand of fellowship was restor[e]d   the meetting dismist   O[tis]. H[obart]. Clerk

19 May 1841

May 19th 1841

The Elders quorum met in the House of the Lord   the fellowship of the quorum was attested   it was voted that President [Amos] Babcock and his counselors ware in good fellowship in the quorum on Thursday evening previous to the confrence to be holden in Kirtland May 22d 1841   O[tis]. H[obart]. Clerk

21 May 1841

May 21th 1841

The Elders quorum met in the House of the Lord   a charge was prefer[e]d by Brother Z[ebedee]. Colt[r]on against Elder Thomas Keer [Kerr]' for unchristian like conduck   the quorum proceded and tried the case Brother Keer made confesion and was forgiven Viz

1th   Brother Keer confest that he was saucy to Brother Colt[r]on   2d that he said that he had Rather receive teaching from Brother [Almon] Babbit than from Brother Colt[r]on because he thought that Brother Babbit knew more but he was unwise in so doing because it hurt his feelings   3d he confest that he had injur[e]d Brother Colt[r]ons feelings in saying that he pretended to know more than he did and did not know half as mutch as he thought he did
O[tis] H[obart] Clerk

22 May 1841

May the 22— 1841

Minuites of a confernce

Held in Kirtland   the cha[i]rman explain[e]d the biesness of the confernce relative to a reorganization   the Elders q[u]arum Elected

Amos Babcok President and Otis Hobert and Thomas Green as
counsellors are unanimously accepted, the members, forty three in
number, ware unanimously accepted also Save the following exceptions viz Lehasa Hollister was rejected but finally accepted Robert
Green[h]algh Ira Bond Justice Blood, to be visited, Phineas Young
David Holman Andrew Hartman Darias Phillips and Solon Bragg
ware rejected

[A more complete account of this conference, reported by William
W. Phelps, was published in Nauvoo in *Times and Seasons* 2 (1 July
1841): 458-60. Because of the relevance of that report to the Elders'
Quorum Record, extensive excerpts are here reproduced.]

[At a general conference of the church of Jesus Christ of Latter
Day Saints, held in Kirtland, Ohio, commencing on Saturday May
22, 1841, Elder Almon Babbitt, being unanimously chosen Chairman and W. W. Phelps, appointed Clerk.—The solemnities began
with singing and prayer. The chairman explained the business of the
conference relative to a reorganization, and resigned his office of
president of this stake, that the conference might express its full
right, and choose its own officers from head to foot. Adjourned one
hour.
Met purusant to adjournment, and opened with singing and prayer.
Appointed a committee of three viz: Thomas Burdick, Zebidee Coltrin and Hiram Winters, to examine candidates for ordination.
The chairman read the several acts incorporating the Church of
Christ of Latter Day Saints in Kirtland, together with a code of by-
laws, which were accepted and adopted unanimously.
Elder Babbitt was then nominated for the president or presiding
elder of the stake in Kirtland; but he declined, yet, after some discus-
sion, was unanimously elected. Elder Babbitt nominated for his
counsellors Elders Lester Brooks and Zebidee Coltrin, who were
unanimously elected.
Thomas Burdick was nominated and unanimously elected Bishop of
Kirtland. He nominated Elders Hiram Winters and Reuben McBride
for counsellors, who were unanimously elected. The president's
counsellors, bishop and his counsellors were then ordained to their
several offices.
The High Priest quorum, Hiram Kellogg, president, and John

Knapp and Joseph Pine, as counsellors, were unanimously accepted by the conference.— The members of the quorum, consisting of six, were also unanimously accepted, save Martin Harris who had one vote against him.

The Elders' quorum, Amos Babcock, president, and Otis Hobart, and Thomas Green as counsellors, were unanimously accepted: The members, forty three in number, were unanimously accepted also; save the following exceptions, viz: Lehasa Hollister was rejected but finally accepted, Robert Greenhalgh, Phineas Young, Justice Blood, (to be visited) Ira Bond, David Holman, Andrew Hartsman Darias Phillips, and Solon Bragg, were rejected.

Adjourned till 10 o'clock, A. M. tomorrow morning.

Sunday May 23. Met pursuant to adjournment. Opened with singing and prayer.

Elder Babbitt delivered a discourse on baptism for the dead, from 1 Peter 4:6, to a very large audience, setting forth that doctrine as compatible with the mercy of God, and grand council of heaven.

After an hour's intermission, Elder W. W. Phelps continued the same subject from 1 Corinthians 15:22, bringing scripture upon scripture to prove the consistency of this doctrine, as among the economy of God and powers of salvation.

Elder Brooks and Adams bore testimony to the truth of what had been advanced as self-evident and self important to let the prisoners go free: after which the sacrament was administered. Adjourned till 8 o'clock to-morrow. A.M.

Monday, May 24. Met pursuant to adjournment. Opened with singing and prayer. Minutes read.

The committee on ordinations reported two candidates for the high priesthood; three for the office of elder; one for priest and one for teacher.

After finishing the business of the elders quorum, it was resolved unanimously, that, as W. W. Phelps had been received into standing and fellowship, by the church at Nauvoo, Ill., he be also received into the same standing and fellowship, according to his "anointing" by the church at Kirtland, and that he receive a letter of commendation from this conference, as he is about to visit the churches east.

Nehemiah Greenhalgh as president and James Crumpton and John Craig as counsellors were elected to preside in the lesser priesthood, and ordained. Resolved that the bishop organize the remaining two quorums of teachers and deacons hereafter. . . .

The several quorums and whole conference, by a unanimous vote, accepted and resolved to uphold the first presidency at Nauvoo, Ill.

Elder Brooks, Morton, and Norton, were appointed a committee to draft a set of bye-laws for the preservation of the Lord's House.

The committee reported a set of resolutions, which appoint two door keepers: that no person shall occupy the pulpits or stand unless entitled by office or invited; that if any person shall deface the said house, they shall be punished according to law: that we will claim our right, and be protected in our worship according to law: that no person shall be allowed to wear his hat on his head in the inner court: and that means be taken to prevent persons from defiling the inside of the house with tobacco cuds and tobacco spittle, and to prevent smoking. . . .

Resolved that the members of either quorum shall not go out to preach unless recommended. . . .

During the sittings of the conference, the greatest harmony prevailed. About 25 baptisms took place, the most of which were for the dead.

Almon Babbitt, Chairman
W. W. Phelps, Clerk.]

10 July 1841

July the 10, 1841

The qu[o]rum of Elders met in the uper part of the Lords house meting opened by prayer by President [Amos] Babcock   at the op[e]ning of the me[e]ting Some observations wer[e] made by Elders [Zebedee] Coltrin and Babcock   then motion was made for to adjourn un till five o clock   the Elders voted for the adjornment

11 July 1841

July the 11

The qu[o]rum met at 12 o clock in the lords House   me[e]ting open[e]d by pray[e]r   a charge was prefer[e]d by Ira Ovi[at]t against Fluellen Knapp for de[a]ling disonestly with him and for Slandering his charicter and then they proceded to he[a]r the testimony   the quorum d[e]cided that Brother Knapp was not guilty of dishonestly

in his deal with brother Ovid But that he was guilty of Slandering Br
Ovit for which he receves the censure of the quorum

11 July 1841

July the 11— 1841

The Elders qu[o]rum met in the Lords house at five o clock   the
me[e]ting was open[e]d by prayer and then proceded to b[u]isness   a
charge pefer[e]d by Elders [Lester] Brooks and [Zebedee] Coltrin[1]
against Elder [Thomas] Kerr for charging them with actual transgression and for calling upon them to repent pubklickly in the Lords
house at the time of worship on the first day of the week   after an
investigation of the marter it was voted that Brother Kerr was out of
order on the last Sabauth and that he make a publick confesion of
the Same

---

[1]Brooks and Coltrin were counsellors in the Kirtland Stake Presidency.

23 July 1841

July the 23, 1841

The qu[o]rum met in the uper part of the Lords house   meting
open[e]d by pra[y]er by Elder [Lester] Brooks   Fluelin Knapp
presented brother [Moses R.] Norris for ordination   it was [a]
unanimous vote except one   the Pres [Amos Babcock] proceded to
ordain him and cal[l]ed on Elder Brooks and [Hiram] Kellogge and
[John] Morton and they ordained him

John Norton Cl[erk]

ther[e] was a motion made at our last confernce for a commity to go
and make certain Elders a viset and they went   brother [Ira] Bond
came and made Satisfaction to the quorum   the hand of fellowship
was with drawn from Robart Green[h]alch as an Elder

John Norton Clerk

8 August 1841

August the 8, 1841

The quorum of Elders met in the Lords House   Brother Lewis
Boothe and Abels Owens wer[e] ordain[e]d to the office of Elders

under the hand of Elders Almon babbit Hiram Kellougg and Elder
[Lester] Brooks & president [Amos] Babcock voted that Br Henry
Mo[o]re be not consider[e]d to belong to ~~belonge~~ the quorum of
Elders

Voted that Robart Green[h]alch be not consider[e]d a member of
the quorum of Elders   Brother Almond babbit prerfer[e]d a charge
[against] Br [Lehasa] Hollister for spe[a]king things before difernt
members of the church that was calculated to injure his influence
and if rece[i]ved would prijudice the brethren against ~~him~~ me[1]
Brother Hollister plead not Gilty to the charge   Brother Babitt was
permited to Sustain his charge by proof   Brother Babitt proceded to
prove the items and after brother Babitt braut [brought] on his
testimony brother Hollister cal[le]d for an ajor[n]ment and it was
granted to him untill the 29 of August and then put over untill the
first day of October by brother Babbitt

---

[1]Unbeknowns to Almon Babbitt (or to the Saints in Ohio), Babbitt had been
disfellowshipped at a General Conference in Nauvoo on the 2nd of October, 1841, for his
zeal in preaching that the Saints should gather at Kirtland instead of Nauvoo. See 12
September 1841, note 1.

5 September 1841

September the 5, 1841

The quorum of Elders met in the uper part of the Lords House
according to apointment   the meting was opend by prayr by Elder
John Norton and then proceded to bisness   President [Amos] Babcock gave Some instructions on the teachings that was in Kirtland
and Sho[w]ed it was verry important for the Elders to come to an
under Standing So as to all teach one thing   Brother Paul Harris
was recommended by the Priest quorum to the Elders quorum as a fit
Brother fo[r] to be ordained in to the Elders quorum and it was voted
that he Shou[l]d be ordained to the office of an e[l]der   President
Babcock and his councillors & Elder [Hiram] Winters proceded to ordain him   it was voted that the meting Shou[l]d be ajornd untill five
a for the purpose of instruction and information and to come to an
under ~~sand ding~~ Standing of the truth

John Norton Clerk

12 September 1841

Sept the 12, 1841

The quorum met acording to apointment and the meting was opend by pray[e]r by Pres. [Amos] Babcock and then proceded to bisness   ther[e] was remarks made by Pres Babcock ~~by~~ on the Elders teaching the places of gethering and he Sho[w]ed that Kirtland [was a] place of gethering for the Saints in the last days[1] and that Nauvoo was Also a place of gethering for the Saints   the Elders Spoke on the Same principel and manifested by ther[e] unanimos Speking that Kirtland was a place of gethering for the Saints ~~ther was aplace~~ vote it was unanimaus agreemment with the Elders that Kirtland was a place of gethering except brother Barns[2]   meting ajo[u]rn[e]d

---

[1]Notwithstanding the many attempts to dissuade the Saints from settling in Kirtland, Ohio (after Nauvoo, Illinois, had been established), some continued to do so (see, for example, *Times and Seasons* 1 [December 1839]: 29). Not only was the Kirtland temple a strong point of attraction, but also many of the Saints were from the Kirtland area. Furthermore, some of the elders, especially Almon Babbitt, were preaching that Kirtland remained a place of gathering for the Latter-day Saints. By the fall of 1840, there was a sizable branch of members living there. In the spring of 1840, Oliver Granger had been sent to Kirtland as the Prophet's attorney-in-fact to cancel his outstanding debts and "free the Lords House from all incumbrances" (Joseph Smith to Granger, July 1840, cited in Jessee, *Writings of Joseph Smith*, p. 475). Additionally, Granger was to "act as president of the Church in Kirtland" until all of his business was completed. So when Kirtland continued to "flourish," despite counsel to the contrary, the leadership at Nauvoo appointed Almon Babbitt to preside as stake president there. (Apparently, Oliver Granger would have received this appointment had it not been erroneously publicized that he was returning to Illinois.) In May, 1841, the brethren at Nauvoo renewed their efforts to encourage gathering to the west, and officially instructed the leaders in eastern Ohio to discontinue the Kirtland stake (see *Times and Seasons* 2 [1 June 1841]: 434). In August 1841, Oliver Granger died at Kirtland and the Prophet sent Babbitt a letter of attorney to take Granger's place. This authorization together with Babbitt's own desire to build up Kirtland led him to encourage the members to remain there. When the Prophet learned that Babbitt refused to stop preaching the gathering to Ohio, Babbitt was disfellowshiped and the Saints in Ohio were instructed to move posthaste to Illinois (*Times and Seasons* 2 [15 October 1841]: 577, and *History of the Church*, 4:443-44). In the meantime, Reuben McBride, of Kirtland, was sent a letter of attorney to manage Church properties in Ohio and Babbitt's power was revoked (*History of the Church*, 4:443-44). When the Kirtland members learned of the firm decision of the brethren in Nauvoo to terminate the stake, Lester Brooks and Zebedee Coltrin, counselors in the stake presidency, wrote to Joseph Smith and requested that the stake continue for a while longer. Realizing the sincerity of these members, the Prophet finally agreed to their proposal in December 1841: "[A]s it appears that there are many in Kirtland who desire to remain there, and build up that place, and as you have made great exertions according to your letter, to establish a printing press, and take care of the poor . . . you may

as well continue operations according to your designs . . . but do not suffer yourselves to harbor the idea that Kirtland will rise on the ruins of Nauvoo" (*History of the Church*, 4:476). Thus the stake in Kirtland continued for a few months longer.

[2]Perhaps this is Lorenzo D. Barnes, who was then travelling east in preparation for his mission to England.

19 September 1841

September the 19. 1841

Th[e] quorum met acording to apointment in the uper part of the Lords House   meting open by Singing and pray[e]r by the President [Amos Babcock] and then proceded   the Elders Spoke on difernt Subjects and the principel of the[i]r being united ther[e] was a motion made [that] the Elders Shou[l]d meet three times a week untill Confernce[1] and the Elders voted for the Same Tu[e]sday friday and Sunday Evenings ware the time for meting closed by pray[e]r

John Norton Clerk

---

[1]Conference had been scheduled for Saturday, 2 October 1841.

2 October 1841[1]

[Conference commenced pursuant to adjournment. Elder Almon Babbitt was unanimously chosen chairman and Elder W. W. Phelps, appointed clerk. The solemnities were opened with singing and prayer.

Resolved unanimously that Elder Jeremiah Knight, Samuel Phelps, and Edwin Cadwell, be appointed a committee to examine candidates presented for ordination.

The chairman then read the 2nd section of the 2nd part of the book of Doctrine and Covenants, explained the relative situation of Kirtland as connected with the gathering of the last days; and laid before the conference, for consideration, the most important items of business—to wit: to aid the poor—for without charity our professions were vain; our gatherings were vain; our teachings were vain, and *our religion was vain*; "Pure religion and undefiled before God and the Father, is this, to visit the fatherless and widows in their affliction, and to keep *ourselves* unspotted from the world,{"} &c. &c.

To be more careful in the selection of competent Elders to preach

the gospel in cities and towns of notoriety, that the cause may continue to triumph, though met be Demetriuses, Alexanders, Simon
Maguses, and many seven sons of Sceva.

And to establish a press at Kirtland, the more effectually to promulgate the gospel; as it is already well known that the press can
spread the principles of religion farther and faster, through the
medium of mail, than the orator in the pulpit. Many other topics
were alluded to, for instruction. Adjourned for one hour.

Met according to adjournment, and opened with singing and
prayer.

Resolved that John Morton be appointed clerk of the church at
Kirtland till next conference.

Resolved that Almon Babbitt as chairman, and Lester Brooks as
clerk, be appointed to sign licenses of the official members of the
branch or stake of the church; and that W. W. Phelps be appointed
recorder to record said licenses.

Resolved that money be raised to purchase a horse and waggon
for the use of the bishop in gathering for, and distributing to the
poor.

Resolved that Elders Samuel Phelps, Hugh Cole, and John
Gaylord, be appointed a committee to travel, in the adjacent branches, and collect alms for the poor.

On the subject of the press at Kirtland—to promulgate the principles of pure religion, as well through the medium of the press, as
the pulpit, and the more advantageously to aid our brethren of the
Church of Jesus Christ of Latter Day Saints, in the great gathering of
these last days; and the better to overcome error with truth, and evil
with good; and to assist the saints to add to their faith, virture,
knowledge, temperance, patience, godliness, brotherly kindness, and
charity; and to help spread the everlasting gospel, as well as warn
this world of woes and wars to come; to note passing events; to give
more light upon the plan of salvation, and to bring the "strong
reasons" to show that the second coming of Christ, to reign upon the
earth, is near.

Resolved unanimously, that Thomas Burdick, the bishop of
Kirtland, and his counsellors, be, and they are are hereby constituted
a company, to establish a press at this place, to be owned in shares of
from ten to one hundred dollars, by the subscribers, and that the said
subscribers are to receive annually, from the said establishment, for

the use of said press and type, such sums as shall be equal to the un-paid interest of the money actually paid and vested in said establish-ment.— And what ever is donated, is to be held in trust and managed by the said company, for the benefit of the Church of Jesus Christ of Latter Day Saints. And said company shall publish a religious periodical entitled THE "OLIVE LEAF,"

Resolved unanimously that the saints in this and the adjacent branches be solicited to lend their aid to carry the above resolution into eff[e]ct without delay.

The proceedings of the Elder's quorum was received and ac-cepted, and instructions given to the committee on ordinations, after which the conference adjourned till to-morrow morning at 10. There was preaching in the evening].

---

[1]These minutes are not part of the Kirtland Elders' Record, but because of their im-portance to this document they have been included here. They were published in the Nauvoo *Times and Seasons* 3 (1 November 1841): 587-88.

3 October 1841

Oct 3rd 1841

The quorum of Elders met persuant [to] apointment in the Lords [house]— meeting open[e]d by Singing & pray[e]r by the first Coun-cil[or] [Otis Hobart] who deliver[e]d a Short adress The meeting was then given to the Elders to devote to any remarks might be made— the Elders from a distance ocupide much time by remarks the clerk then re[a]d the recomends & report from the com-ittee of ordination— Br [John] Numan [Newman] was then ordained & receved into the Elders quorum the meeting then adjourned un-till the 5th [of October]

[A more complete account of this meeting is found in *Times and Seasons* 3 (1 November 1841): 588-89, from which the following has been extracted:]

Sunday Oct. 3rd
[Met pursuant to adjournment. Elder Babbitt deliver{e}d a discourse on the subject of the gathering to a very crowded house. Adjourned

for one hour. Met and Elder Phelps delivered a discourse on "Dispise not prophesyings." The bishop addressed the audience in behalf of the poor, and in aid of the printing establishment.
Adjourned.
Evening Session; opened with singing and prayer.... The committee on ordinations, reported one for the office of the high priesthood; one for the office of an elder, and one for the office of priest, viz. Samuel Phelps, J. Newman, and Daniel Carpenter.
The representation of churches showed an increase of branches and members, but omitted for the sake of brevity.— The remainder of the evening was occupied by Elder Brooks who gave a discourse on the restoration of the kingdom of Israel, (Acts 1,6.)]

5 October 1841

The quorum of Elders met agreeable to[1]

---

[1]The record ends here.

Biographical Appendix

Biographical Notes

J. ACKERLY (probably *John Ackerley* or *Akerley*) (1815-?). Born in Jefferson Co, NY. Ordained elder 29 Jul 1838. Seventy endowed in Nauvoo Temple Jan 1846.

Jaman ALDRICH. Received blessing for working on Kirtland Temple 1835.

William ALDRICH (also *Aldridge*) (1807-1876). Native of Lisbon, Grafton Co, NH. Migrated to Jackson Co, MO. Lived in Kirtland about 1836 to 1838. Stockholder in Kirtland Safety Society 1837. Returned to MO by 1838. Expelled. Moved to IL. After most Saints moved west, settled in Spring Prairie, Walworth Co, WI. Served as bishop in Reorganized Church 1866-1873.

Joseph Stewart ALLEN (1810-1889). Born at Whitestown, Oneida Co, NY. Participated in march of Zion's Camp 1834. Settled in Clay Co, MO. Visited Kirtland 1836. Ordained elder 24 Sep 1837. Moved to Far West, MO. Expelled. Moved to IL. Served as high councilor in Lima, Hancock Co, IL. Migrated to UT, settling in Manti, Sanpete Co, UT. Died in Huntington, Emery Co, UT.

Mathew ALLEN (1800-?). Born at Peru, Clifton Co, NY. Ordained elder 21 Dec 1836. Resident and land owner at Kirtland 1837-1838.

Martin Carrol ALLRED (1806-1840). Born in Warren, KY. Participated in march of Zion's Camp 1834. Received anointing or special blessing in Kirtland Temple 14 Apr 1836. Received into elders quorum same day. Moved to Caldwell Co, MO Fall 1836. Expelled winter 1838-1839.

Sampson AVARD (1800-?). Native of St. Peter, Isle of Guernsey, UK. Baptized 1835. Secured elder's or missionary license in Kirtland 31 May 1836 and anointing in Kirtland Temple 3 Apr 1837. Moved to MO by 1838. Became a leader of retaliatory group known as Danites. Excommunicated after implicating Church leaders as members of this group. Resided in IL 1850.

Almon Whiting BABBIT (also *Babbitt*) (1812-1856). Born at Cheshire, Berkshire, MA. Baptized 1833. Participated in march of Zion's Camp

1834. Ordained seventy 1835. Migrated to northern MO 1838. Expelled. Settled in Nauvoo. Called by Church leaders to rebuild Kirtland 1841. Disfellowshipped 2 Oct 1841 for teaching and promoting building up of Kirtland as "place of gathering." Made satisfaction and returned to IL 1842. Participated in battle of Nauvoo 1846. Moved to UT. Elected delegate to Congress for provisional State of Deseret. Appointed secretary of UT Territory 1852. Died in NE while returning from Washington, D.C.

Erastus BABBIT (also *Babbitt*) (1793-1879). Born at Adams, Berkshire Co, MA. Resident of Kirtland 1835-1838. Blessed for working on temple 1835. Served as president of teachers quorum 1835. Stockholder in Kirtland Safety Society 1837. Ordained elder 29 Jan 1838. Became member of Reorganized Church. Died at Buffalo, Scott Co, IA.

Amos BABCOCK (1808/9-1846). Native of Fort Ann, Washington Co, NY. Moved to Kirtland about 1835. Received elder's license 28 Sep 1836 and anointing in Kirtland Temple 3 Apr 1837. Set apart as president of elders 11 Nov 1840. Seventy endowed in Nauvoo Temple Jan 1846. Died at Winter Quarters, Douglas Co, NE.

E. BADGER (probably *Ephraim Badger*) (1802-?). Born at Waterford, Caledonia Co, VT. Shareholder in Kirtland Safety Society 1837. High Priest endowed in Nauvoo Temple Jan 1846. Resident of Salt Lake Co, UT by 1851.

Jesse BAKER (1778-1846). Born at Charleston, Washington Co, RI. Approved to be ordained elder 11 Jan 1837. Shareholder in Kirtland Safety Society 1837. As elder signed constitution of Kirtland Camp 1838. Migrated to MO 1838. Expelled. Moved to IL. Sustained councilor in elders quorum in Nauvoo 1841. High priest endowed in Nauvoo Temple Dec 1845.

Blake BALDWIN. Resident of Kirtland about 1835-1838. Received blessing for working on temple 1835. Ordained elder 27 Mar 1836. Ordained seventy Jan 1837. Received anointing in Kirtland Temple 25 Jan 1837. Signed articles of Kirtland Safety Society 1837.

Charles N. BALDWIN (1815-1867). Born in Wilna, Jefferson Co, NY. Approved for ordination office of elder 4 Jan 1837. Subscribed to the Kirtland Camp Constitution 1838. Living in northern MO during expulsion of Mormons from that state.

Michael BARKDULL (also *Barkdall*) (1798-1839). Born at Somerset Co, PA. Probable resident of Kirtland 1835. Received anointing in Kirtland Temple 26 Mar 1836 and elder's license 23 May 1836. Died at Quincy, Adams Co, IL.

William BARKER. Resident of Kirtland 1833-1838. Received blessing for working on Kirtland Temple 1835 and anointing in Lord's House 30 Apr 1836. Shareholder in Kirtland Safety Society 1837.

Brother BARNES (possibly *Lorenzo Dow Barnes*) (1812-1842). Born at Tolland, Hampton Co, MA. Participated in march of Zion's Camp 1834. Ordained seventy 1835. Received elder's license 31 Mar 1836. Called to serve in the high council at Adam-ondi-Ahman 1837. Served many short-term missions 1833-1838. Expelled. Settled in Nauvoo. Instructed to leave immediately for mission to England 31 Aug 1841. Died while serving mission in Bradford, England, probably first missionary to die while serving in a foreign land.

James BARNHAM (also *Barnum*) (c1798-?). Received anointing in Kirtland Temple 16 Mar 1836.

Jeremy BARTLETT. Born at Simsbury, Hartford Co, CT. Baptized 1836. Received elder's license in Kirtland 19 Sep 1836.

Reuben BARTON (c1812-?). Ordained elder 27 Feb 1836. Received anointing in Kirtland Temple 2 Mar 1836 and elder's license in Kirtland 31 Mar 1836. Ordained seventy 1837.

Alva (also *Alvah*) *BEMAN* (also *Beaman*) (1775-1837). Born at New Marlboro, Berkshire Co, MA. Friend of Joseph Smith at time of translation of Book of Mormon. Conference held in his home at Avon, Livingston Co, NY 17 March 1834. While in Kirtland, called to temporarily fill vacancy in high council of MO so a full quorum might participate in reception of special blessings in temple 13 Jan 1835. Called and ordained president of elders quorum 15 Jan 1836. Died in Kirtland while serving in that capacity.

Hiram BEMIS (or *Beris*). Ordained elder 22 Oct 1837.

Elias BENNER (?-1838). Joined march of Zion's Camp 11 May 1834 in northern OH. Received elder's license at Kirtland 31 Mar 1836. Ordained seventy 1836. Killed by mob at Haun's Mill.

Asa BILLS. Ordained elder 8 Dec 1837.

Charles BIRD (1803-1884). Born at Roxbury, Sussez Co, NY. Resident of Kirtland 1837-1838. Ordained elder 6 Dec 1837. Signed Kirtland Camp Constitution 1838. Migrated to MO. Expelled and settled in Nauvoo. Seventy endowed in Nauvoo Temple Jan 1846. Died at Mendon, Cache Co, UT.

Isaac Hyde BISHOP (1804-?). Born at Greece, Monroe Co, NY. Resident of Kirtland 1836-1838. Received elder's license 16 Jun 1836. Ordained seventy 1836. Served on high council at Kirtland 1836. Shareholder in Kirtland Safety Society 1837. Called as counselor to stake president at Springfield IL 1840.

Aseph (also *Asaph*) *BLANCHARD* (1800-1879). Born at Hamilton, Madison Co, NY. United with elders quorum of Kirtland 24 Sep 1837. Left Kirtland and traveled to MO with Kirtland Camp 1838. Expelled. Settled in IL. Served mission to MI 1839. Endowed in Nauvoo Temple Feb 1846. Migrated west with pioneers 1852. Died at Springville, Utah Co, UT.

Walter M. BLANCHARD (1804-?). Born at Hamilton, Madison Co, NY. Received patriarchal blessing in Kirtland 1837.

Newman Greenleaf BLODGETT (1800-1882). Born at Chelsea, Orange Co, VT. Resident of Kirtland about 1836-1839. Received elder's license 18 Mar 1838. Probably expelled from MO 1839. Moved to IA. Resident of Nauvoo early 1840s. Died at Ogden, Weber Co, UT.

Justin (also *Justice*) *BLOOD* (1807-?). Born at Orleans, Grover Co, VT. Signed Kirtland Camp Constitution 1838. Ordained elder 22 Jul 1838. MO petitioner.

Ira BOND (1798-1887). Born at Caldwell, NJ. Converted to Mormonism by Joseph Young after moving to Mendon, NY. Settled in Kirtland 1834. Continued to live in Kirtland throughout 1840s. In 1835 received a blessing for working on Kirtland Temple. In 1836 called to preside over deacons quorum. Stockholder in Kirtland Safety Society 1837.

Amasa BONEY (also *Bonney*) (?-1865). Born at Auburn, Cayuga Co, NY. Ordained elder 27 Mar 1836. Ordained seventy 1836. Resident of Kirtland 1837. Stockholder in Kirtland Safety Society 1837.

Lewis BOOTH (also *Boothe*). Ordained elder 8 Aug 1841.

Edmund BOSLEY (1776-1846). Born at Northumberland Co, PA. Moved to Kirtland 1833. Received blessing for working on Kirtland Temple 1835 and anointing 25 Jan 1837. Invested in Kirtland Safety Society 1837. Migrated to MO by 1838. Expelled. Settled in Nauvoo, IL. High Priest endowed in Nauvoo Temple Dec 1845. Died at Winter Quarters, NE while traveling west with pioneers.

Joshua K. BOSLEY (c1810-?). Resident of Kirtland 1836-1838. Ordained elder 18 Mar 1836. Migrated to UT by 1850.

William Bull BOSLEY (1818-1842). Son of Edmund Bosley. Born at Lovinia, Livingston Co, NY. Received blessing for working on Kirtland Temple 1835 and elder's license 4 Apr 1836. Ordained elder and then seventy 1836. Served many short-term missions 1836-1839. Stockholder in Kirtland Safety Society 1837. Moved Daviess Co, MO by 1838. Expelled. Called as president of Geneva (Morgan, IL) stake 1 Nov 1840. Died at Nauvoo.

Abram (also *Abraham*) *Dodge BOYNTON* (1814/15-1865). Born at Newbury, Essex Co, MA. Baptized 1832. Ordained elder 24 Sep 1837. Signed Kirtland Camp Constitution 1838. MO petitioner. Resident of Nauvoo by 1841. Seventy endowed in Nauvoo Temple Jan 1846. Living in UT 1852. Probably owned first store in Bountiful, Davis Co, UT.

James BRADEN (also *Bradin*) (1801-1881). Born at W. Bethleham, Washington Co, PA. Received anointing in Kirtland Temple 26 Mar 1836. Five days later received elder's license. Expelled from MO. Died at Woodpine, Harrison Co, IA.

Solon BRAGG. Resident of Kirtland 1837. Received anointing in temple 3 Apr 1837.

Richard BRASHIER (also *Brasher, Brazier*) (1822-?). Received blessing for working on Kirtland Temple 1835 and anointing in that building 31 Mar 1837. Stockholder in Kirtland Safety Society 1837. As elder left Kirtland with Kirtland Camp July 1838. Left that body in Sep to stay temporarily with friends living at Huron, IL, a few miles west of Springfield. Elder endowed in Nauvoo Temple Feb 1846.

Zephaniah (also *Ziphronia*) *H. BREWSTER* (1797-?). Received blessing for working on Kirtland Temple 1835. Signed Kirtland Camp Constitution and moved to MO 1838. Migrated to UT by 1851.

Phineas BRONSON (c1803-?). Received anointing in Kirtland Temple 26 Mar 1836 and elder's license 8 Jun 1836.

George Washington BROOKS (1808-1887). Native of Jefferson, MS. Participated in march of Zion's Camp 1834. Ordained elder 1835. Received elder's license at Kirtland 31 Mar 1836. Signed Kirtland Camp Constitution and migrated to MO 1838. Migrated to UT, settling in St. George. Died in Gonzales Co, TX.

Lester BROOKS (1802-1878). Born at Lanesboro, Franklin Co, MA. Settled at Madison, Lake Co, OH. Land owner at Kirtland 1837. Received anointing in Kirtland Temple April 1837. Migrated to MO by 1838. Expelled. Returned to Kirtland and resident there 1841-1843. Called to be councilor in stake presidency serving with President Almon W. Babbitt and councilor Zebedee Coltrin 22 May 1841. Died at Buffalo, NY.

Albert BROWN (1807-1901). Born at Windsor, Hartford Co, CT. Ordained elder 25 Jan 1836. Received elder's license at Kirtland 5 Apr 1836. Following marriage at Kirtland 1839, moved to Nauvoo. High priest endowed in Nauvoo Temple Dec 1845. Migrated west with pioneers, remaining in IA for several years during that long trek. Died at Salt Lake City, UT.

Benjamin BROWN (1794-1878). Born at Queensbury, Washington Co, NY. Resident of Kirtland 1836-1838. Served mission to NY and Canada 1836. Ordained seventy Feb 1837. Migrated to MO. Expelled. High priest endowed in Nauvoo Temple Dec 1845. Migrated west with pioneers. Bishop of fourth ward in Salt Lake City, UT and died in that city.

Norman BUELL (1805-1872). Born at Lorraine, Jefferson Co, NY. Baptized and received patriarchal blessing 1836.

Thomas BURDICK (1795-?). Native of Canajorharie, Montgomery Co, NY. Received blessing for working on temple 1835, an anointing in temple 1 Jan 1836 and elder's license 16 Apr 1836. Called to serve as treasurer of elders quorum 9 Nov 1836. Personal property tax payer in Kirtland 1842-1845.

Harrison BURGESS (1814-1883). Native of Putnam, Washington Co, NY. Participated in march of Zion's Camp. Resident of Kirtland 1834-1838. Served mission to OH 1836. As seventy signed Kirtland Camp Constitution 1838. Settled in IL. Crossed plains and died at Pine Valley, Washington Co, UT.

George BURKET (also *Burkett*) (1788-1871). Born at Bedford, Bedford Co, PA. Baptized 1831. Moved to Jackson Co, MO in early 1830s. Expelled by mobs. Settled in Clay Co. Received into elders quorum and anointing in Kirtland Temple 14 Apr 1836. Received elder's license 18 Apr 1836. Moved to Caldwell Co, MO by 1838. Resident of Nauvoo. High priest endowed in Nauvoo Temple Dec 1845. Died at Eden, Weber Co, UT.

Josiah BUTTERFIELD (1795-1871). Born at Dunstable, Middlesex Co, MA. Baptized 1833. Moved to Kirtland about 1834. Served mission to ME and VT 1834, 1836. Received blessing 1835 for working on temple, anointing 1 Jan 1836, and elder's license 4 Apr 1836. Approved for ordination to office of elder 28 Dec 1836. Ordained seventy 1836. Stockholder in Kirtland Safety Society. Ordained president of First Quorum of Seventy 6 April 1837 and served on high council of Kirtland in that same year. After moving to MO and subsequently to IL, served as mission president in MA 1844. Excommunicated 7 Oct 1844. Rebaptized. High priest endowed in Nauvoo Temple Jan 1846. Remained in midwest during 1850s. Baptized member of Reorganized Church 1865. Died at Watsonville, Santa Cruz Co, CA.

Thomas Jefferson BUTTERFIELD (1811-1890). Born at Farmington, Kennebec Co, ME. Shortly after joining Church 1835, moved to Kirtland. Received special blessing in temple. Ordained seventy 1838. Traveled west with Kirtland Camp and settled in Daviess Co, MO 1838. Expelled. Located about three miles west of Nauvoo. Migrated across plains, arriving in Salt Lake Valley 1848. One of first settlers of Fort Herriman, Salt Lake Co, UT. Resided there until death.

William Farrington CAHOON (1813-1893). Son of Reynolds Cahoon. Born at Harpersfield, Astabula Co, OH. Participated in march of Zion's Camp 1834. Ordained into first quorum of seventy 1835. Received blessing for working on Kirtland Temple 1835 and elder's license 20 May 1836. Stockholder in Kirtland Safety Society 1837. Joined other Latter-day Saints as they moved to MO and IL. Seventy endowed in Nauvoo Temple Dec 1845. Died at Salt Lake City, UT.

Anson CALL (1810-1890). Born at Fletcher, Franklin Co, VT. Land owner in Kirtland 1837-1838. Ordained elder 8 Oct 1837. As seventy traveled west with Kirtland Camp 1838. Beaten by mobsters in MO. Expelled. Settled in IL. High priest endowed in Nauvoo Temple Dec 1845. Died at Bountiful, Davis Co, UT.

Samuel CANFIELD. Moved to Kirtland about 1834. Received blessing for working on Kirtland Temple 1835. Received anointing in temple 25 Jan 1836. Stockholder in Kirtland Safety Society. Apparently did emigrate from Kirtland with most Saints 1838. Resident of Kirtland 1840-1841.

John Button CARPENTER (1810-1880). Born at Adams, Jefferson Co, NY. Participated in march of Zion's Camp 1834. Received anointing in Kirtland Temple 3 Apr 1837. Stockholder in Kirtland Safety Society 1837. Migrated to MO about 1838. Expelled. Returned to Kirtland. Resident tax payer in that community 1843. Endowed in Nauvoo Temple 1846.

Daniel CARTER (1804-1887). Native of Benson, Rutland Co, VT. Land owner at Kirtland 1837. Migrated to Daviess Co, MO by 1838. Expelled. Settled in IA, across from Nauvoo. Migrated west with pioneers. Died at Bountiful, Davis Co, UT.

Luman CARTER (1795-?). Born at Benson, Rutland Co, VT. Moved to Kirtland about 1834 and continued to reside in that community until after 1850. Received blessing for working on Kirtland Temple 1835. Taught "vocal music" in temple 1837. One of original shareholders in Kirtland Safety Society.

William CARTER (c1798-c1884). Probably born in OH. Probably baptized and ordained elder before June 1831. Served mission to MO 1831. Received blessing for working on Kirtland Temple 1835. Ordained elder 8 Oct 1837.

Jacob CHAPMAN. Participated in march of Zion's Camp 1834. Ordained seventy 1835. Received elder's license 31 April 1836. Migrated to MO by 1838. Expelled. Returned to Kirtland.

Alexander CHENEY. Served as scribe in elders quorum Jan-Feb 1838.

Elijah CHENEY (1785-1863). Born at Great Barrington, Berkshire Co, MA. Served mission to NY 1833. Stockholder in Kirtland Safety Society 1837. Migrated to MO by 1838. Expelled. High priest endowed in Nauvoo Temple Jan 1846. Died at Centerville, Davis Co, UT.

Nathan CHENEY (1811-1852). Born at Chesterfield, Cheshire Co, NH. Resident of Kirtland about 1836-1838. Stockholder in Kirtland Safety Society 1837. Moved to MO with members of Kirtland Camp 1838. Expelled. Settled in Nauvoo. Seventy endowed in Nauvoo Temple Jan 1846. Died at Centerville, Davis Co, UT.

Orin CHENEY. Resident of Kirtland 1837-1838. Ordained elder 22 Oct 1837. Migrated to MO with Kirtland Camp 1838.

Rodman CLARK. Ordained elder 22 Jan 1838. Ordained seventy 1837. Presented claims against MO. Resided in Nauvoo 1841-1847.

William Oglesby CLARK (1817-1912). Son of Timothy B. Clark. Born at Madison, Jefferson Co, IN. Received into elders quorum 14 Apr 1836. Received anointing in Kirtland Temple 14 Apr 1836 and elder's license 22 Apr 1836. Moved to Clay Co, MO mid-1830s. Resided in Caldwell Co late 1830s. Expelled. Lived in IL early 1840s. Seventy endowed in Nauvoo Temple Jan 1846.

Isaac CLEAVELAND (1780-1860). Born at Watertown, Jefferson Co, NY. Received blessing for working on Kirtland Temple 1835. Shareholder in Kirtland Safety Society 1837. Ordained elder 8 Oct 1837. Migrated to MO about 1838. Expelled. Moved to Nauvoo. Served mission in IL 1839. Died at Sullivan, Ashland Co, OH.

David CLOUGH (also *Cluff*) (1795-1881). Born at Nottingham, Rockingham Co, NH. Migrated from Durham, New Hampshire to Willoughby, OH about 1831. After residing in that community for several years moved to Kirtland. Received blessing for working on Kirtland Temple 1835, anointing in Lord's House 2 Mar 1836, and elder's license 21 May 1836. Ordained elder 28 Feb 1836. Ordained seventy Dec 1836. Stockholder in Kirtland Safety Society 1837. Resident of Nauvoo 1841-1846. Migrated west with Mormon pioneers. Died at Central, Graham Co, AZ.

Joseph COE (1785-?). Probably born in NJ. Baptized and ordained elder before Jun 1831. Served missions to MO and NY 1831. Moved to Kirtland about 1832. Ordained high priest by Joseph Smith 1 October 1832. Assisted in laying foundation stones for Kirtland Temple. Received blessing for working on that building 1835. After being excommunicated Dec 1838, continued to live in Kirtland. Died in that community.

Zera Smith COLE (1805-1886). Native of Middlebury, Addison Co, VT. Participated in march of Zion's Camp 1834. Ordained seventy 1835. MO petitioner. Died at Salt Lake City, UT.

Zebedee COLTRIN (1804-1887). Born at Ovid, Seneca Co, NY. Joined restored Church Jan 1831. Ordained high priest 17 Jul 1832. Attended school of prophets at Kirtland 1833. Served many short-term missions

1833. Participated in march of Zion's Camp 1834. Ordained president of First Quorum of Seventy 1835. Released from that calling 1837. Stockholder in Kirtland Safety Society 1837. After migrating to Nauvoo 1839, returned to Kirtland. Sustained as counselor in Kirtland Stake presidency 22 May 1841. Returned to Nauvoo about 1842. High priest endowed in Nauvoo Temple Dec 1845. Died at Spanish Fork, Utah Co, UT.

Giles COOK. Resident of Kirtland from about 1834 through 1837. Received blessing for working on Kirtland Temple 1835. Ordained seventy 1836.

John COOLEY (possibly *John W. Cooley*) (1811-?). Born at New Haven, Oswego Co, NY. Resident of Kirtland 1840. Resident of Nauvoo 1841-1846. Seventy endowed in Nauvoo Temple Jan 1846. Resident of Grantsville, Tooele Co, UT by 1860.

Libeus (also *Libbeus*) *Thaddeus COONS* (also *Coon*) (1811-1872). Born at Plymouth, Chenango Co, NY. Baptized 1832. Participated in march of Zion's Camp 1834. Ordained seventy 1835. Served mission to NY 1835-1836. Resident of Kirtland about 1837-1838. Shareholder in Kirtland Safety Society 1837. Migrated to MO by 1838. Expelled. Helped build Nauvoo. High priest endowed in Nauvoo Temple Dec 1845. Died at Richfield, Sevier Co, UT.

Joseph COOPER. Received elder's license at Kirtland 21 May 1836. Moved to northern MO by 1838. Expelled.

J. or I. CORKINS (possibly *Israel Caulkins*) (1766-?). Born in Dutchess Co, NY. Received patriarchal blessing in Kirtland.

Oliver COWDERY (1806-1850). Born at Wells, Rutland Co, VT. After meeting Joseph Smith 1829, assisted in translation of Book of Mormon. Received Aaronic and Melchizedek priesthoods with Prophet 1829. One of three witnesses to Book of Mormon. Served mission to MO 1831 and to eastern states 1836. Received keys of priesthood in Kirtland Temple 1836. After eruption of persecution in Jackson Co, MO 1833, returned to Kirtland and appointed to direct printing office. Ordained Assistant President of the Church 1834. Excommunicated after moving to MO 1838. Rebaptized at Kanesville, Iowa 1848. Died at Richmond, Ray Co, MO.

Warren A. COWDERY (1788-1851). Older brother of Oliver. Born at Poultney, Rutland Co, VT, where he practiced medicine. Baptized before

Nov 1831 and appointed presiding high priest of Freedom, NY 1834. After moving to Kirtland 1836, succeeded Oliver as editor of *Latter-day Saints' Messenger and Advocate* and served as Joseph Smith's scribe. Served on high council of Kirtland 1837. Left Church 1838. Although lived in northern MO for a brief period, returned to Kirtland until death.

Jonathan CROSBY (1807-1892). Born at Wendell, Franklin, MA. Moved to Kirtland about 1836. Ordained elder 27 Mar 1836. Ordained seventy 1836. Migrated with members of Kirtland Camp to MO 1838. Expelled. Moved to Nauvoo. Seventy endowed in Nauvoo Temple Dec 1845. Died in Beaver, Beaver Co, UT.

Robert CULVERSON (also *Culbertson*). Received anointing in Kirtland Temple 25 Jan 1836. Ordained seventy 1836. Moved to Caldwell Co, MO by 1838. Expelled. Resident of Nauvoo by 1842.

Lyman CURTIS (1812-1898). Born at New Salem, Franklin Co, MA. Participated in march of Zion's Camp 1834. Resident of Kirtland by 1836. Received anointing in Lord's House 30 Apr 1836 and elder's license 26 Apr 1836. Migrated to Caldwell Co, MO by 1838. Expelled. Settled in Nauvoo. Endowed in Nauvoo Temple Feb 1846. Died at Salem, Utah Co, UT.

Alpheus CUTLER (1784-1864). Born at Plainfield, Cheshire Co, NH. Baptized 1833. Ordained high priest 1836. Received anointing in the Kirtland Temple 1 Jan 1836 and elder's license 29 Apr 1836. Ordained high priest 29 Apr 1836. Moved to Caldwell Co, MO 1836. Expelled. Moved to Nauvoo where he served as high councilor. Served mission to MO 1839. After death of Joseph Smith, rejected the leadership of Brigham Young and organized the True Church of Jesus Christ.

Reuben DANIELS (c1783-c1868). Probably born at Otis, Berkshire Co, MA. Ordained elder 24 Sep 1837. Traveled to MO with Kirtland Camp 1838. Expelled. Resident of Nauvoo early 1840s. Died at Freedom, Portage Co, OH.

Lysander (also *Licander*) *Mason DAVIS* (1816-?). Born at Reading, Middlesex Co, MA. Approved for ordination to office of elder 28 Dec 1836. Shareholder in Kirtland Safety Society 1837. Served as missionary in NC 1839.

M. C. DAVIS (probably *Maleum C.* or *Marvel Chapin Davis*) (1801-1877). Born at Wardsboro, Windham Co, VT. Moved to Kirtland

1833. Received blessing for working on temple 1835 and anointing in that temple 30 Jan 1830. Ordained seventy 1836. Shareholder in Kirtland Safety Society 1837. Excluded from Second Quorum of Seventy 7 Jan 1838. Died at Seville, Medina Co, OH.

Hiram (also *Hyrum*) *DAYTON* (1798/99-1881). Native of Herkimer, Herkimer Co, NY. Lived in Kirtland 1835-1838. Ordained seventy 1836. Resided in Nauvoo early 1840s. Seventy endowed in Nauvoo Temple Dec 1845. Died at American Fork, Utah Co, UT.

Isaac DECKER (1799-1873). Born at Tycanic, Columbia Co, NY. Resident of Kirtland late 1830s. Received elder's license 23 May 1836 and anointing 4 Apr 1837. Moved to Daviess Co, MO by 1838. Expelled. High priest endowed in Nauvoo Temple Dec 1845. Died in Salt Lake City, UT.

J. DICKSON (possibly *John Dickson*) (1781-?). Born NY. Moved to Canada. Baptized 1836 or 1837. Visited Kirtland 1837. Returned to Canada. Moved to Far West, MO 1838. Expelled. Lived in Hancock Co, IL early 1840s.

David DIXON (1877-?). Born at Leeds, Ontario, Canada. Ordained elder 1 Nov 1837. Resident of De Witt, Carroll Co, MO late 1830s.

Clark DRAPER (?-c1842). Ordained elder 20 May 1838. Resident of Kirtland about 1840-1842.

David C. DRAPER. Resident of Kirtland 1838. Dismissed from elders quorum Fall 1840.

William DRAPER (possibly 1774-1854). Born at Wyoming, Susquehanna Co, PA. Resident of Kirtland 1834-1838. Received elder's license May 1836. Stockholder in Kirtland Safety Society 1837. As high priest signed Kirtland Camp Constitution 1838. Called to be patriarch at Kanesville, IA Apr 1848. Died at Draper, Salt Lake Co, UT.

Zemira DRAPER (1812-1876). Millwright. Born at Crambe Northumberland, Ontario, Canada. Resident of Kirtland 1836-1838. Approved for ordination office of elder 4 Jan 1837. Shareholder in Kirtland Safety Society 1837. As priest signed Kirtland Camp Constitution and migrated to MO 1838. Expelled. Moved to IL. Died at Rockville, Washington Co, UT.

Osman (also *Osmyn* and *Osmond*) *DUEL* (1802-?). Native of Galway, Saratoga Co, NY. Resident of Kirtland 1836-1837. Migrated to MO by 1838. Expelled. Settled in IL. Living in UT in 1860.

Chapman DUNCAN (1812-1900). Born at Bath, Grafton Co, NH. Baptized 1832. Resident of Jackson Co, MO by 1833. Received elder's license at Kirtland 31 Mar 1836. Moved to Adam-ondi-Ahman, Daviess, MO by 1838. Seventy endowed in Nauvoo Temple Jan 1846. Migrated to UT by 1848. Died at Loa, Wayne Co, UT.

John DUNCAN (1780-1872). Born at Acworth, Sullivan Co, NH. Participated in march of Zion's Camp 1834. MO petitioner. Settled in IA after the expulsion of the Saints from MO. Died at Cedar City, Iron, UT.

George DUNN (1812-?). Born at Pompey, Onondaga Co, NY. Received anointing in Kirtland Temple 3 Apr 1837.

Jabez DURFEE (also *Durphy*) (1791-1867). Born at Tiverton, Newport, RI. Resident of Jackson Co, MO by 1833. Ordained elder 29 Apr 1836. Received elder's license in Kirtland 2 May 1836. Returned to MO before 1838. Expelled. Moved to IL. Labored as carpenter on Nauvoo Temple. High priest endowed in Nauvoo Temple Dec 1845. Beekeeper in Springville during 1850s.

James DURFEE (also *Durphy*) (1798-1844). Native of Tiverton, Newport Co, RI. Received anointing in Kirtland Temple 26 Mar 1836. Ordained elder 29 Apr 1836. Received elder's license 4 Jul 1836. Living in Caldwell Co, MO by 1838. Expelled. Settled in Lunia, Adams Co, IL where he died.

Perry DURFEE (also *Durphy*) (1797-1872). Born at Tiverton, Newport Co, RI or in Broadalbin, Fulton, NY. Lived in Wayne Co, OH about 1825-1833. Received elder's license at Kirtland 2 May 1836. Resident of MO 1836-1838. Attacked by mobsters 1838. Expelled. Moved to Hancock Co, IL. High priest endowed in Nauvoo Temple Dec 1845. Died at Savannah, Andrew Co, MO.

Buhias DUSTIN (c1796-1874). Probably born at Enfield, Genesee Co, NY. Resident of Kirtland about 1836-1838. Received elder's license 6 Aug 1836. Shareholder in Kirtland Safety Society 1837. High Priest endowed in Nauvoo Temple Jan 1846.

Lewis EAGER (1791-?). Born at Shrewsbury, Worcester Co, MA. Resident of Kirtland 1837-1838. Secured elder's license 1 Apr 1837. Stockholder in Kirtland Safety Society 1837. Ordained elder 29 Jan 1838. As seventy signed Kirtland Camp Constitution 1838. Probably moved to MO 1838. Expelled. Settled in Nauvoo, IL. Seventy endowed in Nauvoo Temple Jan 1846.

William EARL (also *Earle*) (1805-1874). Born at Newton Falls, Trumbull Co, OH. Resident of Kirtland 1837-1838. Ordained elder 15 Nov 1837. Signed Kirtland Camp Constitution and migrated to Daviess Co, MO 1838. Expelled. Living in UT 1851.

Brother FAULK (possibly *Hiram Faulk*). Ordained elder 11 Apr 1841. Resident of Nauvoo about 1843-1847.

Reuben FIELD. Resident of Kirtland 1836-1838. Ordained an elder 8 Oct 1837. Signed articles of incorporation of Kirtland Safety Society 1837.

Rufus FISHER (1804-?). Born at Palmer, Hamblin, MA. Baptized 1832. Ordained elder 27 March 1836. Received elder's license in Kirtland 14 Apr 1836. Ordained seventy 1836. Resident of northern MO late 1830s. Lived in Nauvoo early 1840s. High priest endowed in Nauvoo Temple Jan 1846. Resident of Springville, Utah Co, UT by 1860.

Thomas (G. or *J.) FISHER.* Probable resident of Kirtland 1835-1838. Received blessing for working on Kirtland Temple 1835. Ordained elder 26 Feb 1838. Signed Kirtland Camp Constitution and migrated to northern MO 1838. Expelled. Married Jane Nyman at Nauvoo, IL 1844.

Hezekiah FISK. Participated in march of Zion's Camp 1834. Resident of Kirtland 1836-1838. Received anointing in Kirtland Temple 25 Jan 1836. Received approval to be ordained an elder 28 Dec 1836. Called to serve as first counselor in elders quorum presidency 8 Jul 1838. Probably died at Nauvoo, IL.

Ira FISK (1801-1868). Son of Hezekiah Fisk. Born at Coventry, Kent Co, RI. Baptized 1833. Resident of Kirtland 1840-1845. Died at Kaysville, Salt Lake Co, UT.

Sterry FISK (1797-1839). Son of Hezekiah Fisk. Born at Chautauqua Co, NY. Lived in Kirtland about 1835-1838. Received blessing for working on Kirtland Temple 1835. Ordained elder 26 Jan 1836. Shareholder in Kirtland Safety Society 1837. Died at Nauvoo, IL.

King FOLLETT (1788-1844). Born at Winchester, Cheshire Co, NH. Moved to St. Lawrence Co, NY. Lived at Shalersville, Portage Co, OH during early 1820s. Baptized spring 1831 while living in St. Lawrence Co, NY. Moved to Jackson Co, MO by 1833. Driven out by mobs. Resident of Clay Co 1833-1836. Visited Kirtland where he received anointing in temple 25

Jan 1836 and elder's license 31 Mar 1836. Ordained seventy 1836. Lived in northern MO 1837-1838. Imprisoned and driven from the state. Died while living at Nauvoo, IL. Still remembered for funeral oration delivered by Joseph Smith.

Elijah FORDHAM (1798-1879). Native of New York City, NY. Participated in march of Zion's Camp 1834. Received elder's license in Kirtland 1 Apr 1836. Ordained seventy 1836. Expelled from northern MO late 1830s. Healed by Joseph Smith after settling in IA, across from Nauvoo. Later called to serve in high council in IA. High priest endowed in Nauvoo Temple Dec 1845. Died at Wellsville, Cache Co, UT.

Henry FOSMIRE. Resident of Kirtland 1841-1850.

James FOSTER (1775-1841). Native of Hillsboro Co, NH. Participated in march of Zion's Camp 1834. Resident of Kirtland 1836-1838. Received anointing in Kirtland Temple 30 Jan 1836 and elder's license 9 May 1836. Ordained seventy 1836. Ordained one of presidents of First Quorum of Seventy 6 Apr 1837 and was simultaneously a temporary member of Kirtland high Council. One of leaders of Kirtland Camp during trek to MO 1838. Settled in De Witt, Carroll Co, MO. Died shortly after being driven from that state at Jacksonville, Morgan Co, IL.

Samuel FOWLER (1790-?). Born at Williamstown, New London Co, CT. Resident of Kirtland about 1836-1838. Ordained elder 22 Jan 1838. Signed Kirtland Camp Constitution 1838. Migrated to western MO 1838. Expelled. Settled in IL. Called as stake president of Geneva (IL) stake 1 Nov 1840. High priest endowed in Nauvoo Temple Dec 1845.

E. Samuel FRANKLIN. Ordained elder 24 Sep 1837.

Solomon FREEMAN (1790-?). Born at Granville, Hampshire Co, MA. Baptized 1834. Resident of Kirtland 1837-1838. Received anointing in Kirtland Temple 3 Mar 1837. Possibly living in UT 1860.

David FULLMER (1803-1879). Born at Chillisquaque, Northumberland Co, PA. Moved to Richmond, OH 1835. Baptized 1836. Moved to Kirtland about 1836. Ordained elder 22 Feb 1837. Moved to Caldwell Co, MO Sep 1837. Expelled. Settled in Nauvoo. Served on high council and was member of city council in Nauvoo. Crossed plains. Served as president of Salt Lake Stake, member of the legislature of the Territorial government of UT, and treasurer of Salt Lake City. Died at Salt Lake City, UT.

Moses GARDNER (1794-1852.) Native of Hanover, Morris Co, NJ. Lived there until after 1840. Received anointing in Kirtland Temple 2 Mar 1836 and elder's license 31 Mar 1836.

Henry GARRETT (1782-1862). Born in Laurens Co, SC. Resident of Kirtland 1836-1838. Shareholder in Kirtland Safety Society 1837. Died at Jefferson, Cass Co, IN.

John GAYLORD (1797-1878). Born at Luzern Co, PA. Resident of Kirtland 1836-1838. Ordained seventy 20 Dec 1836. Set apart as one of the First Seven Presidents 6 Apr 1837. Excommunicated 13 Jan 1838. Rejoined Church at Nauvoo 5 Oct 1839. Returned to Kirtland March 1840. Called to serve as clerk pro tem of elders quorum. Seventy endowed in Nauvoo Temple Dec 1845.

Salmon GEE (1792-1845). Born at Lyme, New London Co, CT. Baptized 1832. Resident of Madison, OH during most of 1830s. Made frequent trips to Kirtland while living near that town. Taxpayer and land owner in Kirtland 1835-1839. Received blessing for working on temple 1835. Secured anointing, elder's license, and chosen member of second quorum of seventy 1836. Shareholder in Kirtland Safety Society 1937. Set apart as one of the First Seven Presidents of Seventies. Fellowship was withdrawn 6 Mar 1838. Resident of Kirtland 1840. Died at Ambrosia, Lee Co, IA.

Benjamin GIFFORD. Participated in march of Zion's Camp 1834. Received blessing at Kirtland 1835. Ordained elder 25 Jan 1836.

Truman GILLETT (also *Gillet*), *Jr.* (1811-?). Probably born at Schuyler, Herkimer Co, NY. Ordained elder 30 Apr 1836. Received elder's license at Kirtland 23 May 1836. Probable resident of Nauvoo about 1842-1846. Seventy endowed in Nauvoo Temple Jan 1846.

Dean C. GOULD. A non-Mormon participant in march of Zion's Camp. Baptized 13 Jun 1834 during last phase of march west. Ordained elder 26 Jan 1836. Secured elder's license at Kirtland 5 Apr 1836.

John GOULD (1808-1851). Native of Ontario Co, Canada. Called to travel to Jackson Co, MO 1833 with Orson Hyde to inform Church leaders that they should seek redress by law. Expelled 1833. Missionary seeking volunteers for Zion's Camp. Resident of Kirtland 1836-1838. Received anointing in temple, elder's license, and ordained seventy 1836. Ordained President of First Quorum of Seventy 6 Apr 1837. Dropped from that position 3 Sep 1838 and reinstated that same year. Lived in Nauvoo early 1840s. Seventy endowed in Nauvoo Temple Feb 1846. Died at Cooley's Mill, Pottawattamie Co, IA.

William GOULD (1808-?). Native of Rockingham, Windham Co, VT. Resident of Kirtland 1836-1838. Ordained elder 27 March 1836. Received elders' license 28 Mar 1836. Ordained seventy 1836. Moved to MO by

1838. Expelled. Probably settled in IL. High priest endowed in Nauvoo Temple Feb 1846. Migrated to UT by 1851.

Oliver GRANGER (1794-1841). Born at Rutland, Rutland Co, VT. Moved to Portage, Alleghany Co, NY before 1838. Served mission to eastern United States 1834, 1838 and 1839. Resident of Kirtland about 1835-1838. Received anointing in temple (30 Jan), elder's license (29 Apr) and ordained high priest (29 Apr) 1836. Called to serve in high council of Kirtland 1837. Moved to Far West, MO 1838. Called by revelation (8 Jul 1838) to return to Kirtland as Prophet's attorney-in-fact to conduct Church business. Returned to Far West October 1838 and was precluded from continuing program of settling Church business at Kirtland by extermination order. After serving as Church land agent, acquiring property in Lee Co, IA for the Saints, called by Joseph Smith to be president of church in Kirtland and continue program of settling Church financial affairs there 1839. Died at Kirtland while engaged in this work.

Charles GREEN (probably *Charles Lamone Green*) (1802-1879). Born at Otsega, Otsego Co, NY. Lived at Fort Wayne, Allen Co, IN during most of 1830s and early 1840s. Ordained elder 22 Jul 1838. Seventy endowed in Nauvoo Temple Feb 1846. Died at Rabbit Valley, Wayne Co, UT.

Harvey GREEN (1806-1875). Born at Lake Pleasant, NY. Served mission to IL 1834. Anointed in Kirtland Temple and received into elders quorum 14 Apr 1836. Living at Far West, MO 1838. Expelled. Settled at Nauvoo. Migrated to UT 1848. Died at Sacramento, CA.

Thomas GREEN. Possibly born at Cheshire, England 1802. Sustained as second councilor in Kirtland elders quorum 11 Nov 1838. Might have lived temporarily at Kirtland, then moved to Nauvoo. High priest endowed in Nauvoo Temple Jan 1846. Resident of Cache Co, UT by 1860.

Robert GREENALGH (also *Greenalph*). Dismissed from Kirtland elders quorum 2 Jul 1841.

Addison GREENE (1819-1892). Son of John P. Greene. Born at Brownsville, Jefferson Co, NY. Participated in march of Zion's Camp 1834. Ordained elder 25 Jan 1836. Resident of northern MO late 1830s. Died at Newbern, Jersey Co, IL.

Evan Melbourne GREENE (1814-1882). Son of John P. Greene. Born at Aurelius, Cayuga Co, NY. Served as missionary in ME 1834. Resident of

Kirtland 1835-1838. Served as clerk of elder's quorum 1836-1837. Lived at Glasgow and Nauvoo, IL during early 1840s. High priest endowed in Nauvoo Temple Dec 1845. Died at Sevier Co, UT.

John GRIBBLE (1788-1874). Native of Perth, Quebec, Canada. Baptized 1836. Resident of Kirtland 1838. Signed Kirtland Camp Constitution 1838. Endowed in Nauvoo Temple 1846. Died at Payson, Utah Co, UT.

Judah GRIFFITH. Received anointing in Kirtland Temple 26 Mar 1836.

Selah J. GRIFFIN (1799-?). Native of Redding, Fairfield Co, CT. Resident of Kirtland before 1827. Baptized at Kirtland before Jun 1831. Missionary to western MO 1831. Moved to Jackson Co. Served mission to northwestern states. Driven out by mobs Nov 1833. Moved to Clay Co. Visited Kirtland 1835-1836. Received anointing and elder's license in Kirtland 1836. Ordained seventy 1836. Returned to MO. Living in Caldwell Co. at time of expulsion. Moved to Knox Co, IL 1840. Did not migrate west with Mormon pioneers.

Elisha Hurd GROVES (1797-1867). Born at Madison Co, KY. Baptized 1832. Served many short-term missions 1833-1839, specifically IL. Participated in march of Zion's Camp 1934. Ordained high priest in Clay Co, MO 1834. Sustained member of Far West high council 1838. Died in Washington Co, UT.

Samuel HALE (1798-1838/39). Born at Oneida, Madison Co, NY. Rejected for ordination to office of elder 1836. Resident of Kirtland about 1837-1838. Shareholder in Kirtland Safety Society 1837. As teacher signed Kirtland Camp Constitution 1838. Died at Springfield, Sangamon Co, IL.

John HAMMOND (1795-1859). Born at Chelmsford, Essex, England. During late 1820s and early 1830s, resided at Malone, Franklin Co, NY. Resident of Kirtland 1837-1838. Ordained elder 22 Oct 1837. Traveled with Kirtland Camp 1838. Elder endowed in Nauvoo Temple Feb 1846. Died at South Cottonwood, Salt Lake Co, UT.

Jonathan HAMPTON (1811-1844). Native of Gwillinburg, Ontario, Canada. Resident of Kirtland 1836-1838. Ordained elder 27 Mar 1836. Ordained seventy 1836. Settled in northern MO 1838. Expelled. Died at Nauvoo, IL.

Paul HARRIS. Ordained elder from office of priest 5 Sep 1841.

William HARRIS (1803-?). Native of Nova Scotia, Canada. Received anointing in Kirtland Temple 30 Apr 1836 and elder's license 27 Apr 1836. Resident of Far West, MO 1838. Expelled. Living at Nauvoo 1843.

Elias HART (1804-1846/50). Born in Canada. Resident of Kirtland about 1831-1838. Moved to IL 1839. Resident of Pike Co. 1841-1845. Died while crossing plains to UT.

Joel HARVEY (1779-?). Born at Westminster, Worchester Co, MA. Ordained elder 29 Oct 1837. Signed Kirtland Camp Constitution and migrated west with that group but left before group reached Far West, MO.

Ezra HAYES (1800-1844). Born at Burton, Geauga Co, OH. Resident of Burton until after 1832. Died in IL.

Thomas HAYES (also *Heyes*) (c1817-1846). Not the Thomas Hayes who participated in march of Zion's Camp. Ordained elder 25 Jan 1836. Expelled from MO 1838-1839. Probably died at Mt. Pisgah, IA while crossing plains to Great Basin.

Arnold HEALY. Ordained elder 22 Oct 1837. Shareholder in Kirtland Safety Society 1837. Signed Kirtland Camp Constitution 1838.

Reuben HEDLOCK (also *Headlock* and *Hadlock*). Resident of Kirtland 1836-1838. Received elder's license 1 Apr 1836. On 27 Nov 1837 called to serve as president of elders quorum in place of deceased Alvah Beman. Released as president and moved to MO with Kirtland Camp 1838. Resident of Nauvoo during early 1840s. Served as president of British mission 1843-1845.

Stephen HEDLOCK (also *Headlock* and *Hadlock*) (1790-1847). Native of Weare, Hillsboro Co, NH. Resident of Kirtland 1836-1838. Ordained elder 22 Oct 1837. Traveled to MO with Kirtland Camp 1838. Died at Council Bluffs, IA while traveling west with other Mormon pioneers.

Mayhew (also *Mathew*) *HILLMAN* (1793-1839). Born at Chilmark, Dukes Co, MA. Resident of Kirtland 1834-1838. Ordained elder 29 Apr 1836 after serving as president of teachers quorum. Received elder's license at Kirtland 2 Aug 1836. Served on Kirtland High Council 1837. After migrating to western MO, served on high council at Adam-ondi-Ahman 1838. Died at Nauvoo, IL.

Harmon H. HILLS. Ordained elder 28 Dec 1836. Ordained seventy 1839.

Otis HOBART. Sustained as councilor in elders quorum 11 Nov 1840. Also served as clerk for quorum. Resident of Kirtland 1841.

Lehasha (also *Lahasa*) *HOLLISTER.* Received elder's license at Kirtland 18 Jun 1836. Resident of Kirtland 1840s.

David HOLMAN (1808-?). Native of Templeton, Worcester Co, MA. Approved to be ordained elder 1 Mar 1837. Ordained seventy 30 Jul 1837. Persecuted in Caldwell Co, MO 1838. Home in IL destroyed by mobs 1843. Seventy endowed in Nauvoo Temple Jan 1846.

James Sawyer HOLMAN (1805-1873). Born at Templeton, Worchester Co, MA. Resided at Kirtland 1837-1838. Approved to be ordained elder 8 Feb 1837. As seventy moved to northern MO with Kirtland Camp 1838. High priest endowed in Nauvoo Temple Jan 1846. Died at Holden, Millard Co, UT.

Joshua Sawyer HOLMAN (1794-1846). Born at Templeton, Worcester Co, MA. Lived in NY during most of 1820s and early 1830s. Resident of Kirtland 1836-1838. Received anointing in Kirtland Temple 26 Mar 1836. Moved to northern MO by 1838. Expelled. High priest endowed in Nauvoo Temple Dec 1845. Died at Winter Quarters, Douglas Co, NE while crossing plains.

Richard HOWARD (c1814-?). Native of Royalton, Windsor Co, VT. Received anointing in Kirtland Temple 26 Mar 1836 and elder's license 31 Mar 1836. Moved to Caldwell Co, MO by 1838. Expelled. Called to serve on the High Council in IA Territory Oct 1839.

Isaac HUBBARD. Resident of Kirtland 1835-1838. Received blessing for working on Kirtland Temple 1835. Ordained elder 8 Oct 1837. Signed articles of Kirtland Safety Society 1837.

William F. HUNTINGTON (1784-1846). Born at New Grantham, Chesire Co, NH. Converted to Mormonism 1835 while living in NY. Resident of Kirtland 1836-1838. Received elder's license 7 Jun 1836 and anointing 4 Apr 1837. Stockholder in Kirtland Safety Society 1837. Moved to Adam-ondi-Ahman, Daviess, MO 1838. Among first Mormon families to settle in Commerce (Nauvoo). Served on High Council in that community. Died at Pisgah, Harrison Co, IA.

Heman T. HYDE (1788-1867). Native of Manchester, Bennington Co, VT. Participated in march of Zion's Camp 1834. Served mission to northern states 1834. Resident of Kirtland 1835-1838. Called as member of First Quorum of Seventy 1835. Resident of MO by 1838. Expelled. Moved to IA. High Priest endowed in Nauvoo Temple Dec 1845. Died at Salt Lake City, UT.

Amos JACKSON. Resident of Kirtland 1837-1838. Ordained elder 22 Jan 1838. As seventy signed Kirtland Camp Constitution 1838. Migrated to western MO 1838. Living in IA 1848.

Daniel S. JACKSON (1814-1898). Native of Butternut, Otsego Co, NY. Baptized 1836. Resident of Kirtland 1835-1838. Received elder's license 31 Mar 1836. Called as member of Third Quorum of Seventy Jun 1837. Moved to Daviess Co, MO by 1838. Expelled. Settled in IA. Seventy endowed in Nauvoo Temple Dec 1845.

Truman JACKSON (c1802-?). Ordained elder 27 Feb 1836. Received anointing in Kirtland 2 Mar 1836 and elder's license 19 Apr 1836. Called as member of Third Quorum of Seventy Jun 1837.

George Fitch JAMES (1797-1864). Born in MA. Resident of OH 1820. Baptized Jun 1831. Ordained elder 18 Nov 1831. Received anointing in Kirtland Temple 26 Mar 1836. Died at Brownhelm, Lorain Co, OH.

Aaron JOHNSON (1806-1877). Native of Haddam, Middlesex Co, CT. Following baptism 1836, moved to Kirtland. Resided there 1837-1838. Ordained elder 8 Oct 1837. Signed Kirtland Camp Constitution and migrated to MO 1838. Expelled. Moved to Nauvoo. Served on High Council there and was lieutenant in Nauvoo Legion. Headed company of Saints west, arriving in UT 1850. One of first settlers of Springville and served as first bishop in that settlement. Died at Springville, Utah Co, UT.

Joel Hills JOHNSON (1802-1882) Born at Grafton, Worchester Co, MA. Baptized 1831. Resided at Kirtland 1832-1838. Served many short-term missions to OH and NY 1831-1835. Received anointing 30 Jan, elder's license 30 Mar, and ordained seventy 1836. Migrated to MO 1838. Expelled. Settled at Ramus, IL where he served as president of short-lived Ramus Stake. High priest endowed in Nauvoo Temple Dec 1845. Migrated to UT 1848. Died at Johnson, Kane Co, UT.

Hiram KELLOGG (1793-1846). Born at Barkhamstead, Litchfield Co, CT. Prior to his conversion, resided at Sparta, Livingston Co, NY. Received elder's license at Kirtland 6 Jul 1836 and anointing 31 March 1837.

Stockholder in Kirtland Safety Society 1837. Called as president of high priests quorum in Kirtland Jun 1838. Continued to live at Kirtland until his death.

Easton KELSEY (1813-1899). Native of New Lisbon, Otsego Co, N.Y. Probable resident of Kirtland 1836-1838. Ordained elder 28 Dec 1836. Seventy endowed in Nauvoo Temple Jan 1846. Buried at St. George, Washington Co, UT.

Joseph A. KELTING (1811-?). Native of Philadelphia, PA. Resident and deputy sheriff of Hancock Co, IL early 1840s. High priest endowed in Nauvoo Temple Jan 1846.

Benjamin KEMPTON (1814-?). Born in Kennebec Co, MO. Resident of Kirtland 1837-1838. Ordained elder 24 Sep 1837. Shareholder in Kirtland Safety Society 1837.

Thomas KERR (1816-?). Seventy endowed in Nauvoo Temple Jan 1846.

Eleazer KING (1784-1854). Born at Williamstown, Berkshire Co, MA. Prior to conversion to Mormonism, lived at Sunderland, Bennington Co, VT. Resident of Kirtland 1836-1838. Ordained elder 24 Sep 1837. High priest endowed in Nauvoo Temple Jan 1846. Died at Spring City, Sanpete Co, UT.

Lorenzo Don KING (1816-1839). Son of Eleazer. Born at Sunderland, Bennington Co, VT. Approved to be ordained elder 28 Dec 1836.

Fluellen (Flueling, Flewellin) KNAPP (1815-?). Born at Chaester, Washington Co, NY. Resident of Kirtland 1841-1843. Endowed in Nauvoo Temple February 1846.

John KNAPP (c1797-?). Born in Portage Co, NY. Received elder's license at Kirtland 12 Apr 1836. Resident of Kirtland 1830s and early 1840s. Called to organize branch of Church at Nelson, Portage Co, OH, Oct 1841.

Jeremiah KNIGHT. Ordained elder 22 Jul 1838. Appointed by conference held at Kirtland October 1841 to organize branch of Church at Andover, Ashtabula, OH.

Newel K. KNIGHT (1800-1847). Native of Marlboro, Windham Co, VT. Moved with his family to Colesville, NY about 1811. One of first to be baptized into the restored Church. Served mission to western NY 1830-1831. Moved to Thompson, OH May 1831. Led Colesville Branch to Jackson Co, MO summer 1831. Ordained high priest before 3 July 1832. Driven from Jackson Co, 1833. Settled in Clay Co. where he was appointed member of high council July 1834. Arrived in Kirtland spring 1835 and participated in dedication of Kirtland Temple. Received elder's license there 30 Mar 1836. Returned to MO, arriving May 1836. Ordained elder 24 Sep 1837. Appointed to high council in Far West and moved to Nauvoo in 1839. Served on Nauvoo high council. Left Nauvoo with Saints 1846. Died in Knox Co, NE.

Lorenzo (or *Alonzo*) *D. LaBARON* (or *L. Baron, LeBaron*) (c1819-?). Possibly born at Le Roy, Genesee Co, NY. Ordained elder 11 Jan 1837. Ordained seventy 1839. Seventy endowed in Nauvoo Temple Jan 1846. Resident of Springville, Utah Co, UT by 1860.

James LAKE (1790-1874). Native of White Creek, Rensselaer Co, NY. During his boyhood days, his parents moved to Canada. After baptism, moved to Kirtland where he was resident about 1834-1838. Received blessing for assisting in building Kirtland Temple 1835 and anointing 30 April 1836. Moved to Scott Co, IL 1838. Lived in Nauvoo early 1840s. Elder endowed in Nauvoo Temple Dec 1845. Settled in Ogden Valley where he served on high council of Weber Stake. Died at Oxford, Franklin Co, ID.

Abel LAMB (1801-1874). Born at Rowe, Franklin Co, MA. Resident of Kirtland 1837-1838. Received anointing 31 March 1837. Moved to northern MO by 1838. Expelled. Called to be stake president at Mount Hope, IL. High priest endowed in Nauvoo Temple Dec 1845. Died at Cedar City, Iron Co, UT.

Andrew Losey LAMOREAUX (1812-1855). Born at Pickering, York, Ontario, Canada. Baptized in Canada. Migrated to Kirtland where he lived briefly 1838. As elder signed Kirtland Camp Constitution and moved to MO 1838. Expelled. Moved to Nauvoo. Served mission 1839. High priest endowed in Nauvoo Temple Dec 1845. Served as president of French Mission 1853-1855. Died at St. Louis, St. Louis Co, MO, while returning from this mission.

John LAMOREAUX. Ordained elder 26 Feb 1838.

John McCord LAMOREAUX (1779-1849). Native of Philipstown, Putnam Co, NY. Prior to conversion to Mormonism, lived in Scarborough, Ontario, Canada. Probable resident of Kirtland 1835-1838. As elder migrated to MO with Kirtland Camp 1838. Expelled. Returned to Kirtland where he lived 1841-1843. Ordained elder 25 Apr 1841. High priest endowed in Nauvoo Temple Dec 1845. Died at Nauvoo, IL.

John LAWSON (1805-?). Born at Argyle, Washington Co, NY. Received elder's license in Kirtland 14 Nov 1836. Joined quorum 24 Sept 1837. Presided over Ramus Branch (IL) 1841. Endowed in Nauvoo Temple 1846. Resident of Manti, Sanpete Co, UT by 1851.

Lyman LEONARD (1793-1877). Born in Springfield, Hampden Co, MA. Baptized 1832. Resident of Jackson, Clay and Caldwell counties 1830s. Whipped by mob in MO. Ordained elder 28 Mar 1836. Anointed in Kirtland Temple 30 April 1836. Resident of Nauvoo early 1840s. High priest endowed in Nauvoo Temple Dec 1845. Resident of Salt Lake City, UT by 1851.

Moses LINDSLEY. Ordained elder 28 Mar 1836. Received elder's license at Kirtland 18 Apr 1836.

Cornelius Peter LOTT (1798-1850). Born at New York City, NY. Baptized before 1834. Resident of Kirtland about 1836-1838. Received elder's license 1 Aug 1836 and anointing 31 Mar 1837. Moved to Daviess Co, MO by 1838. Expelled. Probably returned to Kirtland 1839. Settled at Nauvoo before 1842. Endowed in Nauvoo Temple 1845. Migrated to UT 1847. Died at Salt Lake City, UT.

Luke LUCKONE. Ordained elder 15 Nov 1837.

John LYONS (1796-?). Born in Prince William Co, VA. Lived at Griffin Run, WV about 1817-1836. Approved to be ordained elder 4 Jan 1837. After conversion to Mormonism, moved to Caldwell Co, MO by 1837. Resided at Nauvoo early 1840s. Probably died in IL.

Jeremiah MACKLEY (c1800-?). Received anointing 26 March 1836 and elder's license 21 May 1836.

John MACKLEY (c1796-?). Native of Adams Co, PA. Received anointing in Kirtland 26 Mar 1836. Received elder's license 21 May 1836. Resident of Nauvoo early 1840s. High priest endowed in Nauvoo Temple Dec 1845. Resident of Provo, Utah Co, UT by 1860.

William MARKS (1792-1872). Native of Rutland, Rutland Co, VT. Resident of Kirtland about 1836-1838. Received elder's license 1 Jun 1836 and served on Kirtland high council. Stake president at Nauvoo 1839-1844.

Served as alderman in that city. After Joseph Smith's death, joined the reorganization and became a leading figure in that movement. Died at Plano, Kendall Co, IL.

Henry MARSDEN. Ordained elder 22 Jul 1838.

Thomas Baldwin MARSH (1799-1866). Born at Acton, Middlesex Co, MA. Baptized 1830 and became physician to the Church. Traveled to Kirtland spring 1831 and during the ensuing five years served as missionary in MO and eastern United States. Lived in MO early 1830s. Resident of Kirtland about 1835-1838. Ordained apostle 26 April 1835. Returned to MO 1838. Appointed president pro tem of Church. Became disaffected fall 1838 and excommunicated for apostasy 17 March 1839. After remaining in MO for eighteen years, traveled to UT and baptized again July 1857. Died at Ogden, Weber Co, UT.

Moses MARTIN (1812-1900). Born at New Lisbon, Grafton Co, NH. Resident of Kirtland 1835-1835. Member of First Quorum of Seventy 1835. Received anointing in Kirtland Temple on 30 January 1836 and elder's license 1 Apr 1836. Served mission to NY 1837. Moved to Caldwell Co, MO by 1838. Expelled. Moved to Nauvoo. Seventy endowed in Nauvoo Temple Dec 1845. Resident of Salt Lake City, UT by 1851.

Edmond (also *Edward* and *Edmund*) *W. MARVIN.* Called to serve as missionary Feb 1834. Participated march of Zion's Camp 1834. Member of Second Quorum of Seventy 1836.

Reuben MCBRIDE (1803-1891). Native of Chester, Washington Co, NY. Baptized 4 March 1834 in presence of Joseph Smith and Parley P. Pratt. On that night the Prophet called for volunteers to redeem Zion. Enlisted and participated in march of Zion's Camp 1834. Resident of Kirtland about 1836-1848. After most Saints emigrated from Kirtland, he became caretaker of temple grounds. Moved to UT before 1850, settling at Springville. Served on Millard Stake High Council and died at Fillmore, Millard Co, UT.

William McCLARY (also *McCleary, McClerry*) (1793-?). Born in Bennington Co, VT. Ordained elder 26 Feb 1838. Left Norton, OH 1838 with Don Carlos Smith, enroute to western MO. High priest endowed in Nauvoo Temple Dec 1845.

Isaac McWITHEY (c1786-1851). Resident of Kirtland about 1836-1848. Received anointing in Lord's House 25 January 1836.

Joel McWITHEY. Resident of Kirtland 1833-1838 and received blessing for laboring on temple 1835. Received anointing in temple 25 Jan 1836 and elder's license 2 Apr 1836. Member of Second Quorum of Seventy 1836. Signed articles of Kirtland Safety Society 1837.

Elam MEACHAM, Jr. Ordained seventy Jan 1837.

Edwin Parker MERRIAM (also *Merrium*) (1803-1842). Born at New Hartford Co, Oneida, NY. Probably lived at Kirtland 1837-1838. Ordained elder 24 Sep 1837. Signed articles of Kirtland Safety Society 1837 and Kirtland Camp Constitution 1838. Called as stake president at Springfield, IL 5 Nov 1840. Died two years later at Nauvoo, IL.

Daniel Sanborn MILES (1772-1845). Born at Sanbornton, Belknap Co, NH. Received anointing 2 Mar 1836. Ordained elder 28 Feb 1836. Probably resident of Kirtland 1837-1838. Stockholder in Kirtland Safety Society 1837. Ordained seventy Dec 1836 and served as one of First Seven Presidents of Seventies from 1837-1845. Signed Kirtland Camp Constitution and moved to Caldwell Co, MO 1838. Expelled. One of first LDS settlers in Hancock Co, IL, where he died.

William MILLER (1814-1875). Native of Avon, Livingston Co, NY. Resided in Kirtland 1834-1838. Ordained elder 27 Mar, received elder's license 18 Apr, and ordained seventy 1836. Signed articles of Kirtland Safety Society 1837. Moved to Caldwell Co, MO by 1838. Endowed in Nauvoo Temple Dec 1845. Died in Provo, Utah Co, UT.

Artemus (also *Artimas, Artemas*) *MILLET* (also *Millett*) (1790-1874). Native of Westmoreland, Cheshire Co, NH. Baptized by Brigham Young 1834. Resident of Kirtland 1834-1838. Received anointing 30 Jan 1836 and elder's license 11 Apr 1836. Served mission to OH 1836. Signed charter of Kirtland Safety Society. High priest endowed in Nauvoo Temple Dec 1845. Died at Scipio, Millard Co, UT.

Nathaniel MILLIKEN (1793-1874). Born at Buxton, York Co, ME. Resident of Kirtland 1834-1847. Received anointing 30 Jan 1836. Member of Second Quorum of Seventy 1836. Signed articles of Kirtland Safety Society 1837. Left Church Jan 1838 and died in OH.

Albert MINER (1809-1848). Native of Jefferson Co, NY. Resided in Kirtland 1832-1838. Received blessing for working on temple 1835. Approved to be ordained elder 11 Jan 1837. Moved to Caldwell Co, MO 1838.

Seventy endowed in Nauvoo Temple Feb 1846. Died at Iowaville, IA, during Mormon migration to Great Basin.

Jessee MONTGOMERY. Ordained elder 12 Aug 1838. Probable resident of Kirtland 1838-1840.

Henry MOORE (1802-?). Born in Dutchess Co, NY. Ordained elder at Kirtland 29 Jul 1838. Resided in Kirtland and Nauvoo early 1840s. Dismissed from elders quorum 8 Aug 1841. Ordained elder at Nauvoo 1843. Seventy endowed in Nauvoo Temple Jan 1846.

George MOREY (1803-?). Born at Pittstown, Monroe Co, NY. Arrived in Kirtland 26 Nov 1835. Received anointing 30 Jan 1836. Moved to Caldwell Co, MO by 1838. Served on high council at Far West. Expelled. Moved to Nauvoo. Joined Reorganized Church.

Laban MORREL (also *Morrell, Morrill*) (1814-1900). Born at Wheelock, Caledonia Co, VT. Resident of Kirtland 1837-1838. Received anointing 3 Apr 1837. Signed articles of Kirtland Safety Society 1837. Died at Junction, Piute Co, UT.

John MORTON (c1816-?). Possibly born in Scotland. Resident of Kirtland about 1836-1841. After serving as first councilor in elders quorum, set apart as president 17 Jun 1838. Released Nov 1840, after being ordained high priest. Possible resident of Midway, Wasatch Co, UT by 1870.

Jacob MYERS (also *Mires*) (1783-?). Ordained elder at New Portage, OH 1835. Received anointing 26 Mar 1836.

Samuel NEWCOMB (1794-1879). Born at Bernardston, Franklin Co, MA. Lived at Kirtland 1835-1838. Received anointing 25 Jan 1836. Signed charter for Kirtland Safety Society 1837. Migrated to UT. Died at Jamesville, Bremer Co, IA.

J. NEWMAN (also *Nunan*) (possibly *John Newman*) (1802-?). Ordained elder 3 Oct 1841. Resident of Nauvoo early 1840s. Elder endowed in Nauvoo Temple Feb 1846.

Freeman NICKERSON (1779-1847). Native of So. Dennis, Barnstable Co, MA. Joined Church Apr 1833. Participated in march of Zion's Camp 1834. Labored as missionary in OH and Canada 1833 and 1835-1836, including special mission to Canada with Joseph Smith and Sidney Rigdon.

Received anointing 16 Mar 1836 and elder's license 1 Apr 1836. Endowed in Nauvoo Temple Dec 1845. Died at Chariton River, IA.

Joseph Bates NOBLE (1810-1900). Native of Egremont, Berkshire Co, MA. Baptized 1832. Member of Zion's Camp 1834. Lived at Kirtland 1834-1838. Called to be member of First Quorum of Seventy 1835. Received elder's license 7 Apr 1836. Signed articles of Kirtland Safety Society 1837. Moved to MO by 1838. Expelled. Moved to Nauvoo. Migrated to UT. Died at Wardboro, Bear Lake Co, ID.

Moses R. NORRIS. Resided at Kirtland 1837-1841. Received elder's license 6 Jul 1836 and anointing 31 March 1837. Stockholder in Kirtland Safety Society 1837. Disfellowshipped Nov 1837. Remained in Kirtland 1838 after most Saints emigrated. Returned to Church and ordained elder 23 Jul 1841.

John NORTON (probably *John Wesley Norton*) (1820-1901). Born at Lisbon, Wayne Co, IN. Baptized 6 Mar 1838. Resident of Kirtland 1841-1843. Served as clerk for elder's quorum fall 1841. Ordained seventy 1845. Seventy endowed in Nauvoo Temple Feb 1846. Died at Panguitch, Garfield Co, UT.

Gideon ORMSBY (1774-?). Probably born at Manchester, Bennington Co, VT. Resident of Kirtland 1834-1838. Received blessing for working on temple 1835. Ordained elder 27 Mar 1837. Received anointing 25 January 1836 and elder's license 27 Apr 1836. Moved to MO 1838. Expelled. Returned to Kirtland where he lived 1840-1842.

Ira OVIATT (1804-1868). Born at Busling, Rensselaer Co, NY. Blacksmith and carpenter. Resided at Kirtland 1840-1842. Moved to Nauvoo. Elder endowed in Nauvoo Temple Feb 1846. Served on high council of Council Bluffs, IA 1846-1851. Migrated to UT 1851. Settled in Farmington, Davis Co, where he lived until his death.

Abel OWEN. Ordained elder 8 Aug 1841. Resident of Nauvoo early 1840s.

J. PACK (probably *John Pack*) (1809-1885). Born at St. John's, New Brunswick, Canada. Baptized 1836 after moving to NY. Ordained elder 1836. Moved to Kirtland. Joined elders quorum 24 Sep 1837. Moved to MO by 1838. Probably expelled. Settled at Nauvoo. Seventy endowed in Nauvoo Temple Dec 1845. Died at Salt Lake City, UT.

Rufus J. PACK (1803-1866). Native of St. John's, New Brunswick, Canada. Baptized 1836. Resided at Kirtland 1837-1838. Ordained elder 24 Sep 1837. Seventy endowed in Nauvoo Temple Jan 1846.

Noah PACKARD (1796-1859). Born at Plainfield, Hampshire Co, MA. Moved to Parkman, Geauga Co, OH about 1817. Baptized 1 Jun 1832. Served mission 1832 and 1835. Ordained priest 3 December 1832 and elder 6 May 1833. Presided over Church at Parkman. Moved to Kirtland 1835. Received blessing for working on temple 1835. Ordained high priest 13 Jan 1836. Received elder's license 30 Mar 1836. Shareholder in Kirtland Safety Society 1837. Served on Kirtland high council 1836-1838. As high priest signed Kirtland Camp Constitution but did not emigrate with camp. Assisted in building Nauvoo Temple. Endowed in that temple Dec 1845. Moved to UT 1850. Died at Springville, Utah Co, UT, after serving as alderman in that city.

John Edward PAGE (1799-1867). Born at Trenton, Oneida Co, NY. Resided at Kirtland 1835-1838. Received elder's license (1 Apr), anointing (30 Nov) and ordained seventy 1836. Missionary in Canada 1836 and 1837. As seventy signed Kirtland Camp Constitution and migrated to MO 1838. Ordained apostle 19 Dec 1838. Moved to IL. Endowed in Nauvoo Temple Dec 1845. Excommunicated 27 Jun 1846. Died in De Kalb Co, IL.

Samuel PARKER (1790-1846). Born at Brunswich, York Co, ME. Probable resident of Kirtland 1837-1838. Ordained elder 1 Nov 1837. Shareholder in Kirtland Safety Society 1837. As seventy signed Kirtland Camp Constitution 1838. Seventy endowed in Nauvoo Temple Dec 1845. Died at Council Bluffs, IA.

William PARKS (also *Parkes*) (1787-1845). Born at Woodbury, Litchfield Co, CT. Ordained elder 30 Jan 1836. Received elder's license at Kirtland 31 Mar 1836. Resident of Nauvoo early 1840s and died in that community.

Warren PARRISH (?-?). Member of Zion's Camp 1834. Missionary in TN 1834, 1836. Resident of Kirtland about 1835-1839. Ordained seventy 1835. Scribe to Joseph Smith 1835-1837. Signed articles of Kirtland Safety Society 1837. Renounced his membership 1837.

Martin Horton PECK (1806-1884). Native of Rehoboth, Bristol Co, MA. Lived at Danesville, VT before 1835. Resident of Kirtland about 1836-1838. Ordained elder 29 Jan 1838. Shareholder in Kirtland Safety Society 1837. Set apart as counselor in elder's presidency 26 Feb 1838.

Signed Kirtland Camp Constitution and migrated to MO 1838. Expelled. Settled at West Milton, Miami Co, OH. High priest endowed in Nauvoo Temple Dec 1845. Died at Salt Lake City, UT.

Isaac PERRY (1807-?). Born at Madison, Madison Co, NY. Kirtland resident 1836-1838. Received anointing 3 Apr 1837. High priest endowed in Nauvoo Temple Dec 1845.

Stephen PERRY (Perrey). Possibly the *Stephen Perry* (1805) born at Chester, Windsor Co, VT. Approved to be ordained elder from office of priest 29 Nov 1837. High priest endowed in Nauvoo Temple Dec 1845. Or the *Stephen Perry* (1818-1888) born at Middlebury, Genesee Co, NY and died in Springville, Utah Co, UT.

William Chadwick PERRY (1812-1893). Native of Madison, Madison Co, NY. Resident of Kirtland about 1835-1838. Received blessing for working on temple 1835 and elder's license 31 Mar 1836. Ordained seventy 1836. Signed Kirtland Camp Constitution 1838. MO petitioner. Moved to Nauvoo. Served as alternate member of high council. Seventy endowed in Nauvoo Temple Jan 1846.

Samuel PHELPS. Received anointing in Kirtland Temple 25 Jan 1836. Ordained seventy 1836. Presided over conference at Millsford, Ashtabula Co, OH. Resident of Kirtland 1840.

Stephen POST (1810-1879). Born at Greenwich, Washington Co, NY. Resident of Kirtland 1835-1837. Ordained elder 27 Mar 1836 and secured license 1 Apr 1836. Ordained seventy 1836. Missionary in MI 1839.

John PULSIPHER. Possibly *John Pulsipher* (1782-1840). Born at Rockingham, Windham Co, VT. Resident of Kirtland 1838. Ordained elder 22 Jul 1838. Signed Kirtland Camp Constitution 1838. Or *John Pulsipher* (1827-?) born at Spafford, NY. Seventy endowed in Nauvoo Temple Jan 1846.

Zerah (also *Zera*) *PULSIPHER* (1789-1872). Born at Rockingham, Windham Co, VT. Baptized 11 Jan 1832. Resident of Kirtland 1835-1838. Received anointing (25 Jan), elder's license (2 Jul) and ordained seventy 1836. Set apart as president of First Quorum of Seventy 6 Mar 1838. A leader of Kirtland Camp 1838. Located in Daviess Co, MO 1838. Expelled. Settled at Nauvoo by 1840. Seventy endowed in Nauvoo Temple Dec 1845. Captain of pioneer company. Resided in Salt Lake City area until about 1861. Moved to southern UT. Died at Hebron, Washington Co, UT.

Robert RATHBURN (also *Rathbun*). Missionary in OH 1831. Blacksmith living in Jackson Co, MO by 1833. Arrived in Kirtland from Zion Nov 1835. Served mission to OH 1835. Received elder's license 31 Mar 1836. Member of Second Quorum of Seventy 1836. Ordained seventy Returned to MO. Survivor of Haun's Mill massacre 1838.

Eli Harlow REDFIELD (1801-?). Native of Killington, Middlesex Co, CT. Resident of Kirtland 1836-1838. Received elder's license 1 Apr 1836. Served on Kirtland high council. Lived at Far West, MO late 1830s. Received endowment in Nauvoo Temple. Resident of Salt Lake City, UT by 1851.

Leonard RICH. Participated in march of Zion's Camp 1834. Resident of Kirtland about 1833-1842 and of Clay Co, MO during mid-1830s. Missionary 1835. Received elder's license 10 Mar 1836. Signed articles of Kirtland Safety Society 1837. Chosen and ordained one of First Seven Presidents of Seventy 28 Feb 1835. Released 6 Apr 1837, having previously been ordained high priest. Left Church Jan 1838.

Sidney RIGDON (1793-1876). Native of St. Clair, Allegheny Co, PA. Restorationist leader living at Mentor, OH when converted to Mormonism fall 1830. Appointed counselor to Prophet in First Presidency Mar 1833. Resident of Kirtland 1832-1838. During absence of Joseph Smith with Zion's Camp 1834, assisted Oliver Cowdery in directing Church affairs at Kirtland. Educational leader in Kirtland. Received elder's license 21 Mar 1836. Moved to Caldwell Co, MO 1838. Imprisoned during Mormon difficulties in MO 1838-1839. Moved to Nauvoo 1839. Excommunicated 8 Sep 1844. Died at Friendship, Alleghany Co. NY.

Ebenezer ROBINSON (1816-1891). Born at Rome, Oneida Co, NY. Baptized 1835 by Joseph Smith. Resident of Kirtland 1835-1838. Ordained elder 29 Apr 1836. Received anointing 30 April 1836 and elder's license 11 May 1836. Member of Third Quorum of Seventy Dec 1836. Shareholder in Kirtland Safety Society 1837. Moved to Far West, Caldwell Co, MO 1838. Moved to Nauvoo. Became member of Reorganized Church after death of Joseph Smith. Died at Davis City, Decataur Co, IA.

George W. ROBINSON (1814-?). Native of Pawlet, Rutland Co, VT. Resident of Kirtland 1837-1838. Replaced Oliver Cowdery as General Church Recorder 17 Sep 1837. Accompanied Joseph Smith to MO 1838. Expelled. Moved to Nauvoo. Became disaffected and left Church by 1842. Died at Friendship, Alleghany Co, NY.

Isaac ROGERS (1794-1880). Born at Hanover, Graften Co, NH. Resident of York, NY from about 1818-1836. Probable resident of Kirtland 1837-1838. Ordained elder 8 Oct 1837. Signed articles of Kirtland Safety Society 1837 and Kirtland Camp Constitution 1838. Died at Evansville, Vanderburgh Co, IN.

George ROSE (c1820). Received anointing in Kirtland Temple 25 Jan 1836. Ordained elder 26 Jan 1836 and received license 1 Apr 1836. Ordained seventy 1837. Possible resident of Ogden, Weber Co, UT by 1860.

Joseph ROSE (1792-?). Born in Orange Co, NY. Received elder's license at Kirtland 6 Apr 1836. Missionary in IN, MO and IL 1836.

Shadrach ROUNDY (1789-1872). Born at Rockingham, Windham Co, VT. Baptized 1831. Ordained elder 16 May 1832. Moved to Kirtland by 1834. Received blessing for working on Kirtland Temple 1835, anointing 25 Jan 1836 and elder's license 16 Apr 1836. Ordained seventy 1836. Moved to MO by 1838. Resident of Nauvoo early 1840s. High priest endowed in Nauvoo Temple Dec 1845. Arrived in Salt Lake Valley Jul 1847. Bishop of Salt Lake Sixteenth Ward 1849-56. Died at Salt Lake City, UT.

John SAWYER. Resident of Kirtland 1838. As priest signed Kirtland Camp Constitution 1838.

Lucius Nelson SCOVIL (Scovill) (1806-1889). Born at Middlebury, New Haven Co, CT. Resident of Mantua, Portage Co, OH before 1830 and of Kirtland about 1837-1838. Ordained elder 8 Oct 1837. Signed Kirtland Camp Constitution 1838. Resident of Nauvoo about 1841-1846. Endowed in Nauvoo Temple Dec 1845. Moved to UT 1847. Died at Springville, Utah Co, UT.

Almon Worthy SHERMAN (1803-?). Native of Monkton, Addison Co, VT. Resident of Kirtland 1833-1837. Received blessing for working on Kirtland Temple 1835, anointing in temple 30 Jan 1836 and elder's license 1 Apr 1836. Ordained seventy 1836. Moved to MO 1837. Expelled. High priest endowed in Nauvoo Temple Dec 1845.

Henry Garlie SHERWOOD (1785-1867). Born at Kingsbury, Washington Co, NY. Ordained elder 1832. Moved to Kirtland from NY about 1832. Received blessing for working on temple 1835 and elder's license 5 Apr 1836. Missionary in OH, KY, TN 1836. Stockholder in Kirtland Safety Society 1837. Moved to MO by 1838. Expelled. Moved to Nauvoo 1839.

Endowed in Nauvoo Temple Dec 1845. Migrated to UT 1847. Died in San Bernardino Co, CA.

Peter SHIRTS (1808-1880). Native of St. Clair, Columbiana Co, OH, where he resided before 1834. Resident of Kirtland 1834-1838. Received blessing for working on Kirtland Temple 1835. Received anointing in temple and into elders quorum 14 Apr 1836 and elder's license 26 Apr 1836. Moved to MO 1838. Settled at Nauvoo before 1843. A leader of Nauvoo Legion and helped build temple. Seventy endowed in Nauvoo Temple Jan 1846. Resident of Sherman, Iron Co, UT by 1851. Died at Fruitland, San Juan Co, NM.

William SHUMAN. Probable resident of Kirtland 1838. Signed Kirtland Camp Constitution 1838. Probably moved to MO 1839.

Nicholas SINGLEY (1791-?). Born in Lehi Co, PA.

Truman G. SLITER. Land owner in Kirtland 1836. Ordained 24 Sep 1837. Stockholder in Kirtland Safety Society 1837. Probably moved to northern MO by 1838.

Aaron SMITH, Jr. Received anointing in Kirtland Temple 2 Mar 1836. Resident of Nauvoo 1842-1845. Might have been the *Aaron Smith* who paid personal property tax in Kirtland 1848.

Asahel (also *Asael*) *SMITH* (1773-1848). Son of Asael Smith and brother of Joseph Smith, Sr. Born at Windham, Rockingham Co, MA. Baptized 1835. Resident of Kirtland 1836-1838. Member of Kirtland High Council 1837. Moved to MO. Expelled. Settled at Nauvoo 1839. Ordained Patriarch 10 Jan 1844 and presiding Patriarch over Church 1849. Died at Salt Lake City, UT.

Hyrum SMITH (1800-1844). Older brother of Prophet. Born at Tunbridge, Orange Co, VT. One of six original members of Church and one of Eight Witnesses. Moved to Kirtland 1831. Served many short-term missions during 1830s. Leader of Zion's Camp 1834. Received blessing for working on Kirtland Temple 1835 and elder's license 30 Mar 1836. Sustained as Assistant Counselor to First Presidency 3 Sep 1837. Moved to MO 1838. Imprisoned 1838-1839. Moved to Nauvoo 1839. Ordained Patriarch to Church and Assistant President 24 Jan 1841. Died in Carthage Jail, Hancock Co, IL.

James H. SMITH (1805-1887). Born at Littletown, Morris Co, NJ. Ordained elder 29 Apr 1836. Received anointing in Kirtland Temple 30 Apr 1836. Died at Los Angeles, CA.

John SMITH (1781-1854). Uncle to Joseph Smith and father of George A. Smith. Born at Derryfield, Rockingham Co, New York. Baptized in 1832. Missionary in OH and MI 1832. Moved to Kirtland 1833. Received blessing for working on Kirtland Temple 1835. Companion to Joseph Smith, Sr. Shareholder in Kirtland Safety Society 1837. Moved to northern MO 1838. Expelled. Settled at Nauvoo 1839. Moved to Utah 1847. Ordained Presiding Patriarch of Church 1 Jan 1849. Died at Salt Lake City, UT.

Joseph SMITH Jr. (1805-1844). Born at Sharon, Windsor Co, VT. Translated Book of Mormon 1827-1829. Received lesser and higher priesthoods 1829. Organized Church 1830. Resident of Kirtland 1831-1838. Presided over Church until his death. Died in Carthage Jail, Hancock Co, IL.

Joseph SMITH, Sr. (1771-1840). Father of Joseph Smith, the Prophet. Born at Topsfield, Essex Co, MA. One of Eight Witnesses. Resident of Kirtland 1831-1838. Ordained Patriarch to Church 1833. Moved to northern MO 1838. Died in Nauvoo, IL.

Warren SMITH (1794-1838). Native of Becket, Berkshire Co, MA. Resided at Amherst, OH before 1834. Resident of Kirtland 1834-1838. Received blessing for working on Kirtland Temple 1835. Ordained elder 22 Oct 1837. Stockholder in Kirtland Safety Society 1837. Served as clerk of elders quorum Feb 1838. Moved to northern MO by 1838. Died at Haun's Mill, Caldwell Co, MO.

Lorenzo SNOW (1814-1901). Native of Mantua, Portage Co, OH. Resided at Kirtland from 1836-1838. Received anointing in Kirtland Temple 3 Apr 1837. Ordained apostle 12 Feb 1849. Followed Saints as they moved to MO, IL, and UT. High priest endowed in Nauvoo Temple Dec 1845. Sustained as President of the Church 13 Sep 1898. Died at Salt Lake City, UT.

Oliver SNOW (1775-1845). Father of Lorenzo Snow. Born at Becket, Berkshire Co, MA. Resident of Mantua, OH early 1800s. Moved to Kirtland 1837 where he joined elders quorum 24 Sep 1837. Moved to Daviess Co, MO by 1838. Died at Walnut Grove, Knox Co, IL.

William W. SPENCER (1808-1892). Native of Walton, Delaware Co, NH. Missionary in eastern states 1835. Resident of Kirtland 1836-1838.

Received elder's license 25 Oct 1836 and anointing in Kirtland Temple 3 Apr 1837. Resided in IA 1840.

Stephen STARKS. Resident of Kirtland 1836-1838. Received anointing 25 Jan 1836 and elder's license 11 Apr 1836. Ordained seventy 1836. Signed Kirtland Camp Constitution 1838.

Henry STEPHENS (also *Stevens*) (1812-1899). Native of Leeds, Ontario, Canada. Ordained elder from office of priest 29 Oct 1837. As seventy signed Kirtland Camp Constitution and moved to MO 1838. Received endowment in Nauvoo Temple. Moved to UT by 1851. Died at Ephraim, Sanpete Co, UT.

Jonathan STEVENS (c1771-1843). Born at Stamford, Fairfield Co, CT. Baptized 1831. Received anointing in Kirtland Temple 25 Jan 1836 and elder's license 1 Apr 1836. Died at Norwalk, OH.

Uzziel (also *Uziel, Urial, Uriel*) *STEVENS* (1796-1838). Born in Litchfield Co, CT. Baptized and ordained teacher 1831. Ordained elder 1835. Received anointing in Kirtland Temple 30 Apr 1836 and elder's license 5 Apr 1836. Missionary in NY 1836. Probable resident of Kirtland 1837-1838. Stockholder in Kirtland Safety Society 1837. Died in Springfield, IL while traveling to MO.

Dexter STILLMAN (1804-1852). Born at Colebrook, Litchfield Co, CT. Resident of Kirtland 1834-1838. Received blessing for working on Kirtland Temple 1835. Ordained elder 27 Mar 1836 and received license 2 May 1836. Member of Second Quorum of Seventy 1836. Moved to northern MO 1838. Expelled. Settled in IA 1840. High priest endowed in Nauvoo Temple Dec 1845.

Christopher STILLWELL. Received elder's license at Kirtland 8 Nov 1836.

Calvin W. STODDARD (1801-1836). Native of Palmyra, Wayne Co, NY. Probable resident of Kirtland 1835-1838. Received blessing for working on Kirtland Temple 1835. Died at Kirtland, Geauga Co, OH.

Harvey STRONG. Ordained elder 3 Oct 1837. Resident of northern MO late 1830s.

William TENNEY, Jr. (1802-1844). Native of Groton, Grafton Co, NH. Before 1835 lived in NH and NY. Baptized 1834. Resident of Kirtland

1836-1838. Received anointing 20 Jan 1836 and elder's license 1 Apr 1836. Member of Second Quorum of Seventy 1836. Lived in Adams Co, IL., 1840-1845. Died at Quincy, Adams Co, IL.

William TENNEY, Sr. Ordained elder from office of priest 29 Apr 1836.

Charles B. THOMPSON (1814-1895). Born at Niscayuna, Schenectady Co, NY. Received elder's license at Kirtland 4 Apr 1836. Probable resident of Kirtland 1838. As seventy signed Kirtland Camp Constitution and migrated to northern MO 1838. Served mission in NY 1840. High priest endowed in Nauvoo Temple Dec 1845. Resided at St. Louis, MO 1847-1862. Died at Philadelphia, PA.

Edward THOMPSON (c1817-?). Native of Livonia, Livingston Co, NY. Approved to be ordained elder 29 Nov 1837. Resident of Nauvoo early 1840s.

James Lewis THOMPSON (1818-1891). Born at Pomfret, Chautauqua Co, NY. Baptized 1833. Participated in march of Zion's Camp 1834. Resident of Kirtland 1836-1838. Ordained elder 26 Jan 1836 and received license 14 Apr 1836. Moved to Nauvoo 1839. Seventy endowed in Nauvoo Temple Jan 1846. Lived at Council Bluff, IA., about 1847-1856. Migrated to UT 1852. Died at Henryville, Garfied Co, UT.

Julius THOMPSON (c1809-?). Born at Goshen, Litchfield Co, CT. Received anointing in Kirtland Temple 16 March 1836 and elder's license 1 Apr 1836. Ordained seventy 9 Apr 1845.

Samuel THOMPSON (1813-1892). Native of Pomfret, Chautauqua Co, NY. Participated in march of Zion's Camp 1834. Received blessing for working on Kirtland Temple 1835. Ordained elder 18 Mar 1836 and received license 14 Apr 1836. Probable resident of Kirtland 1838. Resided in Caldwell Co, MO by 1838. Seventy endowed in Nauvoo Temple Jan 1846. Moved to UT by 1851. Buried at Vernal, Uintah Co, UT.

Ezra THORNTON (1789-1836). Born at Greenfield, Franklin Co, MA. Resided in NY and PA before 1836. Baptized 1833. Temporary resident of Kirtland 1836. Received anointing 25 Jan 1836 and elder's license 4 Apr 1836. Moved to MO 1836. Died at Far West, Caldwell Co, MO.

Martin TITUS. Received into the elders quorum 17 Feb 1837. Called to serve as missionary in VT 1843. Married Mary Ann Baldwin at Nauvoo 9 Mar 1844.

Moses TRACY (1810-1858). Native of Ellisburg, Jefferson Co, NY. Baptized 1834. Moved to Kirtland about 1835. Resident of Far West, MO 1838. Expelled. Resident of Nauvoo 1840-1846. Seventy endowed in Nauvoo Temple Jan 1846. Died at Ogden, Weber Co, UT.

Michal UMANS (Unams). Ordained elder 22 Oct 1837.

Cornelius G. VAN LEUVEN (1805-1886). Probably born at Midland, Ontario, Canada. Resident of Kirtland 1833-1838. Received anointing 21 Mar 1837. As priest signed Kirtland Camp Constitution 1838. Migrated to northern MO 1838. Died at Springville, Utah Co, UT.

Chauncy Griswold WEBB (1811-1903). Native of Hanover, Chautauqua Co, NY. Resident of Kirtland 1836-1838. Ordained elder 27 Mar 1836. Received elder's license 5 Apr 1836. Member of Second Quorum of Seventy 1836. Shareholder in Kirtland Safety Society 1837. Moved to Daviess Co, MO by 1838. Resident of Nauvoo by 1842. Seventy endowed in Nauvoo Temple Dec 1845. Moved to UT by 1850. Died at Salt Lake City, UT.

E. WEBB (probably *Edwin Densmore Webb*) (1813-?). Ordained seventy 1836. Resident of Kirtland about 1837-1842. Served mission to IL 1839. Moved to Racine, WI 1842. Crossed plains about 1850. Living in Salt Lake City, UT 1854.

James WEBB (1777-1845). Born at Hartford, Hartford Co, CT. Resident of Kirtland 1836-1838. Received anointing in Kirtland Temple 25 January 1836 and elder's license 5 Apr 1836. Died at LaHarpe or Nauvoo, Hancock Co, IL.

Lorenzo WELLS. Resident of Kirtland 1836-1838. Received elder's license 1 Apr 1836. Ordained seventy at Kirtland 20 Dec 1836. Shareholder in Kirtland Safety Society 1837. MO petitioner.

Micah (Michael) B. WELTON (1794-?). Born at Watertown, Litchfield Co, CT. Ordained priest 25 Oct 1831 at Orange, OH. Ordained elder 17 Nov 1831. Labored as missionary in eastern OH 1831 and 1832. Resided in Clay Co, MO 1836. Received anointing at Kirtland 26 March 1836 and elder's license 31 Mar 1836. Expelled from MO. Located in Pike Co, IL, 1839. Ordained seventy May 1839 at Quincy, IL. Called on mission to KY 1844. Endowed in Nauvoo Temple Jan 1846.

Oliver WETHERBY (1806-1854). Kirtland resident 1835-1838. Received blessing for working on Kirtland Temple 1835. Ordained elder 22 Jul 1838. Died in Pottawattamie Co. IA.

Reuben C. WETHERBY. Received anointing in Kirtland Temple 26 Mar 1836.

Newel Kimball WHITNEY (1795-1850). Born at Marlborough, Windham Co, VT. Located at Painesville, OH about 1817. Moved to Kirtland by 1822. Baptized Nov 1830. Ordained bishop's agent in Kirtland area 1 Sep 1831. Operated Church store in Kirtland. Received blessing for working on Kirtland Temple 1835. Charter member of Kirtland Safety Society 1837. Moved to St. Louis, MO 1838. Learned of expulsion of Saints, settled at Nauvoo 1839. Arrived Salt Lake Valley 1848. Bishop of Salt Lake Eighteenth Ward. Died at Salt Lake City, UT.

Charles Billings WIGHTMAN (1815-1895). Born at Utica, Herkimer Co, NY. Received anointing in Kirtland Temple 2 Mar 1836 and elder's license 22 Aug 1836. Resided in Caldwell Co, MO by 1837. Resident of Kirtland by 1843 until after 1861. Moved to Payson, Utah Co, UT by 1864 where he died.

Erastus B. WIGHTMAN (1802-1866). Native of German Flats, Herkimer Co, NY. Ordained elder 18 Mar 1836. Received elder's license in Kirtland 22 Aug 1836. Paid personal property tax in Kirtland 1837 and 1847-1850.

William WIGHTMAN (also *Whiteman*) (c1808-?). Ordained elder 27 Feb 1836. Received anointing in Kirtland Temple 2 March 1836 and elder's license 21 May 1836. Resident of Caldwell Co, MO by July 1837. Resident of Nauvoo mid-1840s.

Benjamin S. WILBER (*Wilbur*) (1811-?). Received elder's license at Kirtland 28 Sep 1836. Approved to be ordained elder 28 Dec 1836 and received into elders quorum 28 Dec 1836. Received anointing 3 Apr 1837. Resident of Kirtland 1837-1838. Shareholder in Kirtland Safety Society 1837. Ordained seventy 1837. Signed Kirtland Camp Constitution 1838. Migrated to Daviess Co, MO 1838.

Frederick Granger WILLIAMS (1787-1842). Born at Suffield, Hartford Co, CT. Moved with family to Cleveland, OH about 1799. Worked as pilot on Lake Erie. Located at Warrensville, OH by 1816. Studied medicine and moved to Kirtland by 1830. Baptized and ordained elder Nov 1830. Missionary in MO 1836 and in MI 1834. Ordained member of presidency of High Priesthood 18 Mar 1833. Owner at Kirtland of F. G. Williams and Co. printing establishment and member of committee to arrange the interior of Kirtland Temple. Served as paymaster for Zion's Camp 1834. Moved to

Far West, MO 1837. Dropped from First Presidency Nov 1837 and subsequently excommunicated. Rebaptized about July 1838. Excommunicated again 17 Mar 1839. Expelled from MO 1839. Located at Quincy, IL, 1839, where he died.

John WILLIAMS (possibly *John Benjamin Williams*) (1818-?). Born at Venice, Cayuga Co, NY. Ordained elder 21 Dec 1836. Probable resident of Nauvoo 1840-1842 and resident of Kirtland 1841. Elder endowed in Nauvoo Temple Feb 1846.

Ira Jones WILLIS (also *Willes*) (1812-?). Born at Burn, Albany Co, NY. Received elder's license 14 Nov 1836. Seventy endowed in Nauvoo Temple Jan 1846. Resident of Salt Lake City, UT by 1851.

B. B. WILSON (also *Willson*) (probably *Bradley B. Wilson*) (1806). Born at Milton, Chittenden Co, VT. Resident of Ray Co, MO late 1830s. Expelled. Moved to Nauvoo by 1841. Seventy endowed in Nauvoo Temple Jan 1846.

George Deliverance WILSON (also *Willson*) (1807-1887). Native of Shelburn, Chittenden Co, VT. Received elder's license at Kirtland 11 Apr 1836 and anointing on 4 Apr 1837. Member of Third Quorum of Seventy Jan 1837. Worked as mechanic at Kirtland 1837-1838. Followed Saints to MO, IL and UT. Veteran of Mormon Battalion. Died at Hilsdale, Garfield Co, UT.

H. H. Wilson (probably *Henry H. Wilson*) (1803-?). Born at Milton Chittenden Co, VT. Recommended to be ordained seventy at Far West, MO 28 Dec 1838. High priest endowed in Nauvoo Temple Dec 1845. Resident of Salt Lake Co, UT by 1860.

Lewis Dunbar WILSON (1805-1856). Native of Milton, Chittenden Co, VT. Baptized 1836. Ordained elder 4 Sep 1836 and seventy 24 Sep 1838. Moved to Caldwell Co, MO by Oct 1837. Recommended for ordination to office of seventy Dec 1838. Expelled. Moved to Nauvoo. Member of Nauvoo high council 1839-1846. Moved to UT 1853. Served on high council at Ogden, UT. Died at Ogden, Weber Co, UT.

W. G. WILSON (probably *Whitford Gill Wilson*) (1799-?). Born at St. Albans, Franklin Co, VT. Baptized 18 May 1836. Ordained elder at Kirtland Aug 1836 and seventy at Quincy, IL May 1839. Endowed in Nauvoo Temple Jan 1846. Ordained high priest Aug 1857.

W. W. WILSON (probably *William Wilson*). Signed Kirtland Camp Constitution and migrated to MO 1838. Expelled. Moved to IA by 1840.

Benjamin WINCHESTER (1817-1901). Born at Elk Creek, Erie Co, PA. Baptized 1833. Resident of Kirtland 1833-1837. Marched with Zion's Camp 1834. Received elder's license 14 Apr 1836. Moved to Caldwell Co, MO 1837. Expelled. Moved to IL, where he lived until 1846. Missionary in eastern states 1837. Migrated to UT and settled at Salt Lake City where he lived until his death.

Hiram WINTER (Winters) (1805-1889). Born near Westfield, Washington Co, NY. Settled in Jamestown, NY. Baptized Jun 1833. Member of Zion's Camp 1834. Resident of Kirtland 1833-1837. Ordained seventy at Kirtland 28 Feb 1835. Received elder's license 2 Jun 1836. Moved to Quincy, IL about 1837 and later to Nauvoo. High priest endowed in Nauvoo Temple Feb 1846. Migrated to UT 1852.

Charles WOOD (1792-?). Born at Guilderland, Albany Co, NY. Resident of Kirtland 1836-1837. Received anointing in Kirtland Temple 31 Mar 1837. Moved to MO by 1838 and to UT by 1851.

Daniel WOOD (1800-1892). Born at Kingston, Dutchess Co, NY. Resident of Kirtland 1834-1838. Received anointing in Kirtland Temple 30 Jan 1836 and elder's license 9 May 1836. Member of Second Quorum of Seventy 1836. Signed Kirtland Camp Constitution and moved to MO 1838. Seventy endowed in Nauvoo Temple Jan 1846. Migrated to UT by 1851. Died at Bountiful, Davis Co, UT.

Willard (also *William*) *WOODSTOCK* (1800-?). Served on high council at Kirtland during assembly that approved Doctrine and Covenants as law of Church 1835. Served again on high council at Kirtland Sep-Nov 1837. Shareholder in Kirtland Safety Society 1837. High priest endowed in Nauvoo Temple Jan 1846.

Alexander WRIGHT (1804/1805-?). Born at Marmoch, Banffshire, Scotland. Immigrated to Canada 1835. Baptized 1836. Moved to Kirtland about 1837. Approved to be ordained elder from office of priest 6 Dec 1837. Moved to MO by 1838. Labored as missionary in Scotland 1839-1841. Moved to Nauvoo by 1843. Seventy endowed in Nauvoo Temple Jan 1846. Migrated to UT 1847. Died at Virgin City, Washington Co, UT.

Elisha WRIGHT (1811-?). Born in Glover Co, VT. Ordained elder 28 Dec 1836.

William WYRICK (Wirick). Ordained elder 21 Dec 1836. Ordained seventy 1839. Sold land in Nauvoo 1844-1845.

Gad YALE (c1790-?). Born at Bristol, Hartford Co, CT. Participated in march of Zion's Camp 1834. Resident of Kirtland 1835-1836. Received blessing for working on Kirtland Temple 1835. Ordained elder 26 Jan 1836. Received anointing in temple 30 Jan 1836. Member of Second Quorum of Seventy 1836. Moved to Caldwell Co, MO Fall 1836. Seventy endowed in Nauvoo Temple Dec 1845. Moved to UT by 1851.

Brigham YOUNG (1801-1877). Son of John Young. Born at Whitingham, Windham Co, VT. Resident of Kirtland 1833-1837. Participated in march of Zion's Camp. Ordained apostle 1835. Sustained president of Quorum of the Twelve Apostles 1840 and president of The Church of Jesus Christ of Latter-day Saints 27 Dec 1847. High priest endowed in Nauvoo Temple Jan 1846. Died at Salt Lake City, UT.

John YOUNG (1791-1870). Son of John Young and brother of Brigham Young. Born at Hopkinton, Middlesex Co, MA. Missionary in NY 1835. Member of Second Quorum of Seventy 1836. Resident of Kirtland about 1836-1838 and 1841-1845. Received anointing in Kirtland Temple 25 Jan 1836. High priest endowed in Nauvoo Temple Jan 1846. Migrated to UT by 1851. Died at Salt Lake City, UT.

Lorenzo Dow YOUNG (1807-1895). Native of Smyrna, Chenango Co, NY. Resident of Kirtland 1833-1838. Received blessing for working on Kirtland Temple 1835. Member of Second Quorum of Seventy 1836. Moved to Daviess Co, MO 1838. Expelled. Moved to IL where he lived during early 1840s. Endowed in Nauvoo Temple Dec 1845. Moved to UT by 1851. Died at Salt Lake City, UT.

Phineas Howe YOUNG (1799-1879). Son of John Young and brother of Brigham Young. Born at Hopkinton, Middlesex Co, MA. Methodist preacher prior to his conversion to Mormonism. Given copy of Book of Mormon by Samuel Smith. Baptized 1832. Served many short-term missions in U.S. and Canada 1830s and early 1840s. Resident of Kirtland 1833-1838. Received elder's license at Kirtland 26 Apr 1836. Moved to Nauvoo 1840. Returned to Kirtland before 1845. Endowed in Nauvoo Temple Dec 1845. Died at Salt Lake City, UT.

Sources Used in Preparing Biographical Notes

Published Sources

Andrus, Hyrum L., and Richard E. Bennett. *Mormon Manuscripts to 1846.* Provo, Utah: Harold B. Lee Library, 1977.

Backman, Milton V. Jr., Keith Perkins, and Susan Easton, comps. *A Profile of Latter-day Saints of Kirtland, Ohio and Members of Zion's Camp: Vital Statistics and Sources.* Provo, Utah: Religious Studies Center, 1983.

Bitton, Davis, *Guide to Mormon Diaries and Autobiographies.* Provo, Utah: Brigham Young University Press, 1974.

Cannon, Donald Q. and Lyndon W. Cook. *Far West Record: Minutes of The Church of Jesus Christ of Latter-day Saints, 1830-1844.* Salt Lake City, Utah: Deseret Book Co., 1983.

Easton, Susan, comp. *Membership of the Church of Jesus Christ of Latter-day Saints. 1830-1844.* Provo, Utah: Religious Studies Center, 1984.

Esshom, Frank. *Pioneers and Prominent Men of Utah.* Salt Lake City, Utah: Pioneers Book Publishing Co., 1913.

Jenson, Andrew. *Latter-day Saint Biographical Encyclopedia.* 4 vols. Salt Lake City, Utah: Deseret News, 1936.

Smith, Heman C., and Joseph Smith III. *The History of the Reorganized Church of Jesus Christ of Latter Day Saints.* 4 vols. Independence, Missouri: Herald House, 1951.

Smith, Joseph. *History of the Church of Jesus Christ of Latter-day Saints.* Edited by B. H. Roberts. 7 vols. Salt Lake City, Utah: Deseret Book Co., 1964.

Unpublished Sources

Church Membership File. Genealogical Department. Salt Lake City, Utah.

Family Group Sheets. Genealogical Department. Salt Lake City, Utah.

Journal History. Church Archives. Salt Lake City, Utah.

Kirtland Council Minute Book. Church Archives. Salt Lake City, Utah.

Membership Records. RLDS Church Historical Library. Independence, Missouri.

Minutes, First Council of Seventy, 1835-1841. Church Archives. Salt Lake City, Utah.

Missionaries of The Church of Jesus Christ of Latter-day Saints, 1830-1842. Church Archives. Salt Lake City, Utah.

Nauvoo Temple Endowments. Genealogical Department. Salt Lake City, Utah.

Patriarchal Blessing File. Church Archives. Salt Lake City, Utah.

United States Census Records, primarily 1830-1870. Microfilm copy, Brigham Young University. Provo, Utah.

Date Index

Name and Subject Index

anointed, 17; biographical note, 75

Butterfield, Josiah, anointed, 5; biographical note, 75

Butterfield, Thomas, petition for ordination, 22; biographical note, 75

Cadwell, Edwin, 63

Cahoon, William F., charges Addison Green with unchristian-like conduct, 25; called a liar, 25-26; biographical note, 75

Call, Anson, petition for ordination accepted, 31; ordained, 32; biographical note, 75

Camfield, Samuel, anointed, 4; presented doctrinal question, 24; questioned answered, 25; questioned regarding faithfulness, 38; biographical note, 76

Carpenter, Daniel, 66

Carpenter, John B., anointed, 27; biographical note, 76

Carter, Daniel, ordained, 28; biographical note, 76

Carter, Luman, charges John Gribble with not magnifying office of priest, 41; biographical note, 76

Carter, William, petition for ordination accepted, 31; ordained, 32; biographical note, 76

Chapman, Jacob, one of a committee to visit elders, 53; to visit Ira Bond, 54; biographical note, 76

Cheney, Alexander, anointed, 27; acts as clerk for Elders' Quorum, 37; elected permanent clerk, 39; mentioned, 40; biographical note, 76 Cheney, Elijah, anointed, 4; biographical note, 76

Cheney, Nathan, anointed, 27; biographical note, 76

Cheney, Orin, petition for ordination, 23; ordained, 32; biographical note, 77

Clark, Rodman, ordained, 39; biographical note, 77

Clark, William O., received into quorum and anointed, 17; biographical note, 77

Cleaveland, Isaac, petition for ordination denied, 14; second petition for ordination, 24; petition accepted, 31; ordained, 32; biographical note, 77

Clough, David, anointed 9; petition for ordination accepted, 14; ordained, 17;

biographical note, 77

Coe, Joseph, mentioned, 18; biographical note, 77

Cole, Zera S., mentioned, 48; biographical note, 77

Cole, Hugh, mentioned, 64

Coltrin, Zebedee, charges Thomas Kerr with unchristian-like conduct, 56; counselor in Kirtland Stake Presidency, 57-58; mentioned, 59, 60; requests Prophet to continue Kirtland Stake, 62; biographical note, 77

Comforter, Holy Ghost, 48, 49

Confession, of sins, preparation for endowment of power, 6

Consecration of oil, 8, 11, 27, 28

Cook, Giles, mentioned, 5; biographical note, 78

Cooley, John, mentioned, 52; biographical note, 78

Coons, Libbeus T., mentioned, 8; biographical note, 78

Cooper, Joseph, mentioned, 38; biographical note, 78

Coppentis, John B., mentioned, 14

Corkins, I., mentioned, 19, 22, 23; biographical note, 78

Cowdery, Oliver, record of organization of Elders' Quorum, 2; gives instructions, 6, 7; appointed to write rules concerning licensing elders, 14; clerk of meeting, 15; and plural marriage, 35; biographical note, 78

Cowdery, Warren A., ordains Truman Gillett, Jr., 18; biographical note, 78

Cowdery, William, president of priests' quorum in Kirtland, 2

Crosby, Jonathan, ordained, 16; biographical note, 79

Culverson, Robert, anointed, 4; biographical note, 79

Curtis, Lyman, ordained elder, 18; biographical note, 79

Curtis, Thomas, ordained, 32

Cutler, Alpheus, anointed, 4; ordained high priest, 18; biographical note, 79

Daley, Moses, mentioned, 14

Daniels, Reuben, petition for ordination accepted, 31; biographical note, 79

Davis, Hyland, charged and found guilty

47; one of committee to examine
candidates for ordination, 63;
biographical note, 90

LaBaron, Lorenzo D.,name presented
for ordination, 23; biographical note,
91

Lake, James, anointed, 18; biographical
note, 91

Lamb, Abel, hands laid on for health, 23;
anointed, 28; performs ordination, 28;
one of vigilance committee, 38;
biographical note, 91

Lamoreaux, Andrew, complains of bad
behavior of Joshua Bosley, 43;
biographical note, 91

Lamoreaux, John, ordained, 40;
mentioned, 55, 56; biographical note,
91

Lawson, John, unites with quorum, 31;
biographical note, 92

Leonard, Lyman, request for ordination
approved, 17; ordained, 18; anointed,
18; biographical note, 92

Letters of recommendation, 40

Licensing, policy of, 41

Lindsley, Moses, ordained, 16;
biographical note, 92

Lott, Cornelius P., anointed, 28;
biographical note, 92

Luckone, Luke, recommended for
ordination, 33; approved and ordained,
33; biographical note, 92

Lyons, John, request for ordination, 22;
biographical note, 92

Mackley, Jeremiah, anointed, 13;
biographical note, 92

Mackley, John, anointed, 13; biographical
note, 92

Marks, William, appointed bishop's agent,
30; makes remarks regarding John
Morton's character, 44; performs
ordination, 45; biographical note, 92

Marsden, Henry, received into quorum
and ordained, 47; biographical note, 93

Marsh, Thomas B., publisher of *Elders'
Journal*, 36; revelation received for, 40;
biographical note, 93

Martin, Moses, testifies in trial, 10;
biographical note, 93

Marvin, Edmund W., anointed, 5;

biographical note, 93

McBride, Reuben, blessed, 3; anointed, 5;
counselor in Kirtland bishopric, 57;
receives letter of attorney from Prophet,
62; biographical note, 93

McClary, William, ordained, 40; one of
committee to visit the elders, 53;
biographical note, 93

McWithey, Isaac, anointed, 4;
biographical note, 93

McWithey, Joel, anointed, 4; biographical
note, 94

Meacham, Elam, anointed, 18;
biographical note, 94

Melchizedek priesthood, 47

Merriam, Edwin P., name presented for
ordination, 23; petition for ordination
approved, 31; biographical note, 94

Miles, Daniel S., petition for ordination
rejected, 14; ordained, 17; anointed, 9;
biographical note, 94

Miller, William, ordained, 16;
biographical note, 94

Millett, Artemus, anointed, 5;
biographical note, 94

Milliken, Nathanael, anointed, 5;
biographical note, 94

Miner, Albert, petition for ordination
rejected, 14; name presented for
ordination, 23; biographical note, 94

Mission appointments, 19

Montgomery, Jessee, ordained, 48;
biographical note, 95

Moore, Henry, name presented for
ordination, 46; ordained, 47; charged
with striking his wife, ill-treatment of a
brother, and unwise conduct, 50;
charged with various sins, 51; cut-off
from quorum, 51; disfellowshipped
from quorum, 61; biographical note, 95

Morey, George, anointed, 5; biographical
note, 95

Morrel, Laban, anointed, 27; biographical
note, 95

Morton, John, chosen second counselor in
quorum presidency, 3; organized elders
for anointing, 6,27; mentioned, 13, 21,
31, 34, 41, 42, 45, 46; gives
exhortation, 22; qualifications of, to
assume presidency of quorum, 44;

selected to be president of quorum, 45;
ordained president of Kirtland Elders'
Quorum, 45; calls counselors, 46;
ordains elder, 47,48; proposes quorum
discuss doctrinal topics in quorum
meeting, 48; presides, 49; unites with
high priest quorum, 51; one of a
committee to draft rules for
preservation of Kirtland Temple, 59;
appointed clerk for church at Kirtland,
64; biographical note, 95
Moses, ancient prophet, question
regarding, 24
Murmuring, against heads of Church, 23
Myers, Jacob, anointed, 13; biographical
note, 95
Nauvoo, official place of gathering, 62
Newcomb, Samuel, anointed, 4;
biographical note, 95
Newman, John, ordained and received
into quorum, 65,66; biographical note,
95
Nickerson, Freeman, anointed, 11; joins
quorum, 25; consecrates oil, 27;
anointed, 28; biographical note, 95
Noble, Joseph B., meeting in home of, 13,
16; biographical note, 96
Norris, Moses R., name presented for
ordination, 21; anointed, 28; performs
ordination, 28; name presented for re-
ordination, 60; biographical note, 96
Norton, John, charged with various sins,
50; charge not sustained, 50; performs
ordination, 55; appointed one of a
committee to draft rules for
preservation of Kirtland Temple, 59;
serves as clerk, 60, 61, 63; biographical
note, 96
"Olive Leaf", newspaper proposed at
Kirtland, 65
Olney, Oliver, president of teachers
quorum, 2
Operations, gifts and, of the spirit, 49
Ordinations, priesthood, to be approved
by common consent, 5
Ormsby, Gideon, anointed, 4; ordained,
16; biographical note, 96
Oviatt, Ira, prefers charge against
Fluellen Knapp, 59, 60; biographical
note, 96

Owens, Abel, ordained, 60; biographical
note, 96
Pack, John, unites with quorum, 29, 31;
biographical note, 96
Pack, Rufus, petition for ordination
presented and approved, 31, 38;
biographical note, 97
Packard, Noah, assists in ordination, 48;
gives opinion regarding doctrinal
matter, 49; biographical note, 97
Page, John E., anointed, 5; biographical
note, 97
Parker, Samuel, ordained, 33;
biographical note, 97
Parks, William, ordained, 16;
biographical note, 97
Parrish, Warren, clerk, 15; biographical
note, 97
Partaking, of sacrament, 18
Peck, Martin H., ordained, 39; ordained
counselor in quorum presidency, 40;
mentioned, 41; presides, 42;
biographical note, 97
Perry, Isaac, anointed, 27; biographical
note, 98
Perry, Stephen, approved for ordination
as priest, 35; biographical note, 98
Perry, William, charges Solomon
Nickerson with polygamy, 35;
biographical note, 98
Phelps, Samuel, anointed, 4; charges
Thomas Dutcher with preaching false
doctrine, 51-52; one of committee to
examine candidates for office of elder,
63; to collect money for poor, 64;
approved to be ordained high priest,
66; biographical note, 98
Phelps, William W., appointed clerk of
conference, 57, 59, 63; delivers sermon,
58, 66; received into fellowship, 58; to
record licenses, 64
Phillips, Darias, not in good standing, 57,
58
Pine, Joseph, counselor in high priest
quorum, 58
Plural marriage, 35
Poor, of the church, 29
Post, Stephen, ordained, 16; biographical
note, 98
Preparations, for endowment of power, 26